THE GREATEST STORY NEVER TOLD

THE GREATEST STORY NEVER TOLD

DIANE SWAFFIELD

The Elonias Foundation

Copyright © 2023 by The Elonias Foundation

All rights reserved. No part of this book may be reproduced in any manner whatsoever without written permission except in the case of brief quotations embodied in critical articles and reviews.

First Printing, 2000. This edition, 2023

To Amoen

For if your story was never told, then we would still be asleep to our real selves

To Jason

Who is not only my husband and my best friend, but is someone I remember from another place, another time. Thank you for your love and support so that this story could finally have an ending

Finally

To all who shared my life through the years, I say thank you. Without you I may never have found the truth

Introduction

I have left the hardest part of this story until last .. the Introduction. What I say now will either invite you to begin the story, or place it aside and say "it's not for me". The title of the book defies explanation at this point, except to say .. if you decide to read it, you will never view yourself or life again in the same way.

This story is not for those who have a few hours to spare and who are looking for a fill-in to pass the time. There are many other books on so many subjects that will suffice. This book is different. It is a story of a place that once existed, a very long, long time ago. A place that still exists in the memory that it still does.

From the far distant future back to the far distant past, there was so much to be learnt. Those who were sent back into the far distant past were called "initiates". They have become lost within the Worlds of the past, and have not returned back home.

However, don't be fooled. There is nothing mystical about being an initiate. For an initiate is only someone who has something to learn, and after all .. this story may be about you!

I am not the author of this book, but I held the blueprint for it to be written. That blueprint represents the time when "you" and "I" existed. It is the story of why the future needed to enter back into the past. A story of hope, of love and the promise of a tomorrow where love reigns supreme. Where all is "one" again.

This book took more than four years to complete, from beginning to end. At times months went by without anything at all. Then suddenly, there it was again .. words rushing into my mind, and I could hardly keep up, with my fingers flying over the keyboard at my computer.

With every page I grew more and more aware of the beauty of the journey through life and beyond. All had a purpose. What seemed to be disorder was really order having an experience of an opposite. All had an equal value, and in understanding that everything has to have an opposite to exist, I became more and more aware that everything was in its rightful place.

The Greatest Story Never Told has now been told. It is not a story "before its time". It is a story "right on time". I hope that it opens up your memory to your real self, as it has done to mine.

Chapter 1

THE GREATEST STORY NEVER TOLD

Beyond the lands of long ago, where prophets and sages spoke of great things, there were those who stood in the entrance to the Golden City, welcoming the weary travellers who had finally found their way home. Their skin looked bronze in the golden light as they gently took the hands of those who had crossed the bridge of forgetfulness into the Land of Remembrance.

This was home to all who had ventured into the lower realms where memory through time had been their illusionary master. Their return heralded their success in combating the power of forgetfulness within the illusionary worlds to where they had been.

It was a wondrous sight. The travellers who seemed so battle weary and tired from their journey, were held up by those who had waited so patiently for their return.

Gently they were carried through the Golden Gates to the Temple of Regeneration, where the power of the pure sound would erase their pain and sorrow, and restore them back to their true sound.

What is the purpose to the journey through the Lower Worlds? A question that is often asked of many initiates who have successfully completed the journey. I would like to share the answer with you ... but who am I? I am one who completed the journey, but has returned. Why did I return?

The answer is simple. I have come to look for those who have not returned home yet. They have taken too long .. because they have lost their way!

A sound was sent out .. to call home all who had ventured within the Lands of the Lower Worlds. That sound comes from the centre of the Hidden Lands, also known as the Golden City. It contains a powerful resonance that triggers the memory code of what is "real". It is the point of discovering the illusion of who one believes themself to be. Whether the sound is recognised or discarded, is entirely up to the initiate. The sound is sent out only once. That is why it goes under the name of "the final sound".

And you might ask "what is meant by real?" It is the power point of knowing one's true identity, rather than the image of what one believes themselves to be. The Lower Worlds are composed of thought. Thought being the operative word to describe the fragmented power of memory that governs these Worlds.

When the entry into the Lower Worlds is offered to an initiate, an intense training regime begins through multiple simulation techniques of possibilities and probabilities that will be encountered. Multiple opportunities are offered through an imprint simulator, that formulates the range of testing procedures to be accepted by the initiate to form the basis of one's life.

When this is completed, the initiate is given 7 options to by- pass any or all of the imprint possibilities, through what is called the point of "recall". This is a major factor in the regaining of memory through the consciousness of each initiate who has taken on life in the Lower Worlds.

It is the first stage of remembering the essence of one's being, rather than through the acceptability of one's inheritance through cultural, religious and economic conditioning.

I need to formulate a descriptive portrait of what an "initiate" is. The term, in itself, is not accurate. However, through the language of the uninformed, then this term is somewhat closely aligned to someone who is learning, rather than has learnt.

To learn, one needs to have an opportunity to face many and variable challenges and issues that have never been faced before. Thus, the Lower Worlds have been chosen to be the venue for the appropriation of opportunities for each initiate to encounter.

Exposure to time can be either a hindrance or a valuable example to be understood. More often than not, the initiate acquires a sense of belonging to the sameness of routine and regimented way of life that the inhabitants of the Lower Worlds follow. This being the case, then there are no boundaries to cross, for time has taken its toll on all who delay their journey to embrace the limitedness of what time has to offer. The initiate now stands alone.

The consequences of abandoning one's direction through life, for the limitedness of involvement of life, is to become totally unaware of the true purpose for that life. However, the karmic law of cause and effect plays its hand at variable intervals, so as to re-direct the initiate into a more viable position of remembering.

The empowerment of the singular self is often viewed as the most destructive aspect of the initiate's journey through the Lower Worlds. For within the empowerment of singularity, the collective has been abandoned. The desires within singularity often lead to the need for success, prestige and power. Qualities that are often applauded and encouraged by those who are unable to attain them through their own thoughts and actions, and who desire a mentor to follow.

The Lower Worlds were initially chosen because they held a multitude of opportunities that would filter out any residue energy that could not be supported within the next stage of the initiate's journey.

At this point, I need to speak of "the collective". What is meant by "the collective, and how does it work?" ...

When I speak of "the collective", I am speaking about one aspect of "a collective". The terminology of "the" and "a" would no doubt be confusing in itself. However, to place an accurate description before you, I need to clarify the difference.

The collective has a relationship to a greater part of itself, of which is called a collective. Within the collective there is a central power point. That power point is called The Central Chamber.

It is the nucleus of all experience that has been gathered by all who reside within the collective. It could be likened to a main data bank. This Central Chamber holds resonating isobars of sound that links up with other collectives. Each collective having their own Central Chamber.

It would be easier to describe "the collective" as having multiples of itself on varying frequency ratios. Hence, many collectives connected together through a main corridor. However, I need to offer to you an explanation that would give an accurate account within your framework of understanding, and so I need to firstly introduce you to the power range of thought. For thought is sound. It is a created substance of energy that permits a movement through the space that you occupy. It is the power point to permit an action to originate from. That is simple in itself. However, what is not simple, is the acknowledgement that thought and sound are one and the same.

Within the context of humanity, sound is used to highlight one's feelings. To exemplify one's current response to the circumstances within their life. Sound can become either a friend or foe through the acceptability of that sound or non-acceptability thereof.

Communication is through sound that originates from thought. The emanation of sound transfers thought from one to another via a wave note of energy that is not always audible to the human consciousness. It is however, detectable on the sub-space field of awareness.

If you were able to view sound within the World that you occupy, you would be amazed to see that the space that you occupy is totally immersed in the power of sound, that would be better described as a colour spectrum of light. All thought has a designated destination and a point of origin. What you need to know is that thought, which we have determined is also sound and viewed as a colour spectrum of light, has a powerful influence upon all life everywhere.

However, you cannot have an original thought. For all thought has been pre-ordained for the evolvement for the species of that time/space frame. You need to understand that thought is the holding station of memory. Memory being the main adjudicator of all sound within that point of space.

Within the scope of what can be deemed predictable, memory holds on tightly to all thought, for memory is the main power point of thought. When I speak of it being predictable, then I am merely ascertaining the fact that all memory has within it a power source of needing to locate itself over and over again. I will explain what I mean ..

The source of all thought is the power of memory. Memory being the resource to rely upon to re-live that thought over and over again. However, memory is not reliable when the thought within that memory is relied upon for a reference point of thought. Before you become totally confused by my statement, I will give to you an example:

"An action is taken to compare one thought to another. One person's memory contradicts another person's memory of an event or a place. Each person believes that their memory is accurate. However, no memory is ever accurate, because it is tainted by what has occurred after the event. The person that you were is within the actuality of the event, but not within the memory of the event. For thought through memory is coloured by events after the actuality.

The person having the memory is not the person within the actuality". Thought, therefore, is an ever-changing movement of energy, not regulated by actuality at all, but rather by the re-arrangement of one's response.

So, what is truth? Is it a response to a memory or a response to one's image of actuality? The re-arrangement of truth is through one's response to memory. It is as simple as that. Truth does not exist except through one's need that it does.

Let us look at original thought. What is original thought, and what created it? A simple question that does not have a simple answer. Within the complexity of the answer, lies a multitude of possibilities, for original thought is composed of a multi-layered option for thought to begin and end.

There are 7 options or examples to follow when speaking about original thought. It could be seen as one thought divided into 7 examples of itself. Within those 7 examples there is a power point, or central point that draws each layered example into one relationship to itself via the 7 possibilities.

That is the complexity within the answer. However, for a singular mind to comprehend such an answer is difficult indeed. So I will re-arrange the answer in such a way as to provide a more understandable and definable example for you to follow.

Thought originates from sound. Sound being the central point for all memory to begin and end. Thought is the carrier wave of sound to create the memory. An original thought is an original sound that needs to find a variance of itself through possibilities. Therefore, it is defined through 7 examples of itself, with each moving towards a singular point as each is experienced. Thus, 7 examples being from the one thought, allowing for memory to be the tool to advocate the variation of thought to be possible. Existence is upon 7 layers of thought. Each layer is composed of metatronic sound waves. Each layer is unique in itself, in that it offers a separate opportunity for existence to be explored through possibilities.

The Original thought given over to that layer of thought is what is called "space". Each layer is divisible by itself, so that all possibilities or options are covered. Therefore, there are 7 original thoughts coming from one original sound.

What created original thought? When this question is asked, then there is a need for a beginning and an ending. For original thought to begin, there has to be a point where an ending has begun. If you follow me. Nothing can begin without something ending. All is a movement. Sound can never be viewed as being stationary. For if sound was ever at a point where there was no movement, then it becomes a memory only.

The influx of light is only perceived by one's perception of life. And within this phrase, lies many answers to the most often asked question of all: "What lies beyond life?"

When life is viewed through an absolute rather than abstract perspective, then the question pertaining to what lies beyond life is very pertinent indeed. The answers to this question are not readily acceptable by many, and indeed very few realise the significance within these answers to direct them further afield. The answers would be discarded immediately by those to whom the question has no relevance, except to enhance their objective of their life.

"What lies beyond life?" is more a definition rather than an actual question. There are a multitude of answers to this question than could possibly be covered within this subject at hand. However, I wish to convey a powerful reminder to all who are researching for the formula to existence, and therefore I am listing below some of the main points that need to be recognised and acknowledged.

- There is no purpose to life: it is only the means to recognise the singular aspect of existence, which is the opposite of what is "real". There is no fixed point of reference to recall when observing this fact.
- Life has a blueprint that offers no answers and leads back into itself.
- Beyond the blueprint lies an image of what is possible, but not factual.
- Memory beyond life is only a mirror image of what might have been if life was absolute.
- Beyond the barrier of awareness lies the reality aspect of what is known.

These are only a few examples that I wish to convey at this time. There is no limit to what one is able to remember, and when you ask about remembering, then the pathway of the initiate has only just begun within the Lower Worlds. The need to remember is all that an initiate requires at this point. For within the need, comes the power to remember.

Memory has nothing to do with remembering. Memory being the subjective rather than the objective response to life. To remember is to re-instate what is known but never forgotten. There is a direct link-up with the power range of what is "real", what is true, through the higher sub frame of consciousness. This sub frame holds powerful modules of coding. Each aspect of coding could be likened to a relay stream of data, corresponding with multiple formulas that hold the residue of failed programming processes.

This, in itself, sounds rather complex and unimaginative. However, it is the Main Chamber that needs to be recognised by each initiate before the "real" can be maintained throughout the lower conscious levels, via the personality.

It operates on 6 main frequency waves of sound. Each wave is governed by a "note" that resonates to 122 mega cycles per second. It oscillates through a division of 4 chambers, in order for the full sound to be recognised and re-directed to the higher accord.

The higher accord being the prime directive for all initiates to respond to, relative to their true purpose of entry into the Lower Worlds. All in all, the Main Chamber is the energiser of all sound that each initiate is required to maintain during their sojourn through the Lower Worlds.

The power point of all remembering can be likened to a bridge. A connection point from the illusion to the elusive. Within time, lies the paradox to life. The belief in the fundamental relationship between mind and matter, co-existing with a multitude of opportunities that allow for a learning experience within a limited span of time. Therein lies the difficulty of understanding the "elusive".

What is "elusive" when one is involved in remembering? Surely it is the requirement to initiate a movement away from the image of what one believes life to be, towards the unknown aspect beyond life, whilst still existing within life. This simple example holds the key to finalising the need to believe in the limitedness of all life everywhere.

However, when the first step across the bridge is taken, then the observation point of being disconnected from what is known, so as to enter what is not known, can be totally disconcerting for many. This is due to the fact that the belonging relationship to what is known is very powerful indeed, and detachment from one's image of themselves and life offers no comfort when taking the step from illusion to the elusive. Hence, the elusive is seen through the eyes of they who have not as yet reached the power point of remembering.

To reach towards a goal, an aim, or a centre point of progress, only offers an opportunity, but is not the opportunity at all. For within the very act of reaching, lies the reason for that act, but does not embrace the final outcome, still to be experienced. Therefore, the need to remember is not the power point of remembering, but instead is only the thought that it is possible.

The term illusion to elusive is therefore accurate, when the boundary between the two is clearly defined by one's need to remember. The power of thought within the Lower Worlds is the prime producer of all action. It is the program directive for all life and is closely monitored by the wheel of predictability through the creative laws of matter, rather than the cycle of probability and possibility through the point of what is new.

It holds antiquated aspects of sound that validate and highlight the need to enforce itself through previous examples of itself, thereby re-enacting the program of life over and over again. Thought that does not fit into the category of predictability is quickly eliminated or restructured.

I have placed these examples within this framework of understanding because the power of remembering is not simply the need to remember, but is the core product of an initiate's journey within the Lower Worlds. It is within the code of ethics that the initiate, whilst not having the remembering for the journey at hand, embraces the opportunity of life with the powerful presence of its light.

The test surely is to bring within the Lower Worlds the messenger who does not remember the message, but yet the beauty of the messenger becomes the message instead.

The pathway of the unenlightened is often seen as a destructive pathway to a designated place of suffering. For it is believed that to distance oneself from one's God or Creator is to bring attention to what is its opposite, which is known as the "tempter" or "devil".

Through fear, the Lower Worlds are controlled by the minority who are seen as agents for the God or Creator, and who are able, at will, to designate rules and regulations on "its" behalf. To follow blindly is to show allegiance and the destructive pathway to suffering will be alleviated.

Thought can be viewed through two separate categories. Thought that is derived from the point of observation through the past, and thought that is yet to be observed, but is the main point for what is "real".

The main focus on life is centred through the validation of what is known by the majority. What has already been established as reference for future learning, is regarded as being the "no-go zone" for change. Its motive is clearly defined through the need to regenerate the movement of the past through the hero worship of those that have travelled the learned path and have left their legacy of experience for future generations to follow.

The general consensus seems to be that when one is no longer living, then their many and varied experiences are given greater credence, and are duly spoken of as being "before their time".

References and quotations of their works are then directed onto those who need to remember the greatness of those who dared to speak in terms, contrary to the times in which they lived. For progress and change within the Lower Worlds is not progress or change at all, but rather a shallow example of deploying a different relationship to the sameness, rather than an advanced and progressive outlook on life.

The barriers and boundaries of thought are the restrictive aspects to understanding life, and indeed the purpose to life. They are the invisible restraints within the Lower Worlds, that could be called the "jailers" of evolution. For the limitedness of thought reinforces the wheel of life to continually reproduce a limited movement into a greater awareness. An awareness beyond all thought, that brings with it the power to remember. Not the need to remember, but the power to make it possible.

The Parity Chamber allows for the overflow of new formulas, which is new thought, to infiltrate the structure of life through the recognition that beyond oneself, lies a greater and more profound structure of life. This Chamber holds the residue of all thought that has not been utilised within the framework of that time-frame before.

It is essential that the initiate becomes involved with the formation of new thought through each opportunity that permits an enquiry into the purpose for life. This is only possible if a stalemate exists within the thought pattern of the initiate, thereby triggering a resistance to current trends of thought that are currently being used by themselves and others.

However, it is too easy to adopt the image of change by substituting an opposite thought to take place of an old thought. For within the opposite, lies an element of what one has just forgone. I will give to you an example ..

"To remove the thought of belief from the consciousness, so that no-belief exists, offers up the belief that no-belief exists."

With the recognition that all thought has within it its opposite, is to arrive at the same destination, except facing the other way. The image is still the same, it is just viewed from a different perspective. Thought always has an opposition to itself. For within the structure of thought, lies a definition to define itself.

Whether one uses the order of evaluation to determine one aspect or another, is decided through the need to view oneself via that particular aspect of thought. For example, to desire a better life is to decide that one does not have a life that is desirable. Therefore, through that thought, another thought has been created of what would be ascertained as a better life. The same thought, but viewed through an observation of opposites.

To understand the purpose to one's life is to also understand the purpose of life. No opposite exists. For all is one and the same.

No division exists between the point of remembering and the recognition of always knowing when thought is not ascertained through its opposite.

I have shared these examples with you, so as to provide a valuable tool to remembering, for life is cyclic when choosing an opposite within thought. Whether you face one way or the other, you will eventually come back to the starting point of where you left. All thought being cyclic through the power of memory. Where there is no memory, there is no thought to return to.

How can thought be "new"? Within that question lies an answer that many will fear. A simple answer, and yet the consequences of accepting it into one's life, is phenomenal. It will divide all thought that you have into aspects of denial. Let me explain:

The structure of life within the Lower Worlds is governed by sound. Sound being the main power point of all thought that originates from the creative force, known to many as the Creator or God. A singular deity that generated a powerful order within the Worlds to which you live.

However, to see it as order, is to also see it within disorder. For the singular factor is the main point of conjecture. Multiple species of life operate within a coding structure that permits them to exist either independently or within a bi-partisan arrangement with other species. However, no collective arrangement is recognised, unless illustrated through singularity living within an ordered existence of survival.

Individuality through the program of life allows for a singular sound to be recognised through an identity. This identity revolves around a personality that has been structured to permit life to exist via a component of learning examples. Gender, culture and social influences regulate the personality to either accept or reject the power base of thought through the very power of this influence.

However, the inner memory always exists, and to this point I refer back to the question "How can thought be new?" The answer is to deny all previous thought that does not permit the inner memory to exist. Simple really, except to those who need to depend upon their image of their existence as being the core product of life.

To divide all thought into aspects of denial is to unravel the tapestry of one's life. To unlock the inner chamber of remembering that life is, in itself, only the by-product of the journey "through" life. For life is the opportunity to reveal the echo of the past to the sound of what is "real".

Your question would be "Why does the "real" need to reveal the echo of the past?" and to answer that, I need to share the following:

- Initiates were sent into the Lower Worlds in order toview the power of separation, as opposed to the collective aspect of light.
- To remember what is "real" through the "unreal" is the point of observation of all initiates who are given the opportunity to further their journey beyond the Central
- Within forgetfulness, the true sound of an initiate can be seen and understood.For it is only within forgetfulness, can the true remembering take place.

The resolution of sound is through an ultra-spectrum of light. This light is composed of 16 resolutions. These resolutions are then filtered through a composite of "light streams" that could be called filters of sound. Light streams are the point of impact that all thought originates from.

This statement in itself, has quite an influence on the human concept of thought. Light by itself is unknown, except through the image of what it is. Light to the dwellers of worlds whereby light is given from a fading star system is the light to which they understand. However, even that light contains sound.

Sound being the foundation of all energy, and all energy contains thought. Thought is the Master Coding System of all life. It is composed of neutronic substances that filter out unwanted and discarded energy residue. That residue is then inverted into a past coding system, known as the metatronic system of sound.

A simple analogy would be .. A sound is sent from the Higher Mind which governs all thought, which governs all life. This could be deemed "a program". Within this program lies multiple opportunities for the sound to experience itself. As factions of itself have been experienced, then the break- away pattern of sound, which is thought, is then filtered into a neutral zone, to be eliminated.

The main program of life has many sectional aspects of itself. The resultant image of experience is through a lower mind, which I will call the "self". This "self" is a composite of many experiences through the time zone of that particular program. Many, many separate lives are experienced, with multiple opportunities given to draw from the collective mind of all lives, lived by others.

These are called "imprints", which, of course, are not lived by the one "self".

Familiar concepts exist within the variation of experiences. The "will" to live, rather than survive is often misunderstood. For survival of the species is a coding formula that maintains the strong rather than the weak. However, the "will" to live, is masked through the need to survive, but that is not correct at all. For within the "will" to live lies the awareness factor of existence. To live rather than survive. An interesting point to consider.

Within the Lower Worlds are many variations of programs that exist side by side. The evolutionary aspect of life is not designated one program at all, but rather many programs that are constantly being drawn from. For example, one "self" can draw from up to 8 different programs through one lifetime.

You need to understand that previous life experiences through other time frames and the imprint value of lives all contain valuable experiences, but are often from other program directives. Therefore, a variation of expression is often seen as being contradictory and contrary. The initiate is required to bring multiple programs into one program of expression. Namely, the point of impact is thus seen as the point that all comes into one sound. That sound is then followed through by a more direct thought pattern that allows for the power range of what is "real" to be accessible.

Within the point of observation of one's life, comes the need to understand the direct involvement of a Higher Mind. As given earlier, the Higher Mind is the provider of the sound that governs all life. It is the main programmer that offers multiple opportunities for life to exist within the Lower Worlds on many dimensions. Each dimension being the mainstay for the power range of that frequency of life to exist.

Also, each dimension has its own sound that is totally different from an adjacent dimension, and so on. Therefore, dimensional life is required to exist within the power point of that sound only.

Fractional thought is through the revolution of sound that is not complete in itself. Through the many and varied dimensions comes the need to verify the conversion of one dimension into another, and so on. This is done through fractionalising the power of thought. Not thought within a singular division of itself, but thought being the sound of that particular frequency or junction of space. In other words, each dimension has an access point through a grid network. Each dimension has a ratio of sound that becomes fragmented within the entry point of an adjacent dimension. For within the grid structure of life, therein lies a paradox. This paradox refers to life having an opposite of itself to exist.

The criteria for sound to exist is through the need for life to be divisional, and within each division of life through the network of dimensions, lies the very purpose to its existence.

Sound, being thought, having a multi-divisional experience away from the pure sound of light, from whence it all began.

When I speak of life having an opposite of itself to exist, I will explain. For within the building blocks of life, lies two formulas. One being the formula for existence, and the other being the formula for break-away patterns of that existence to exist. For within the clarity of experience, there is an opposite thought to allow it to be viewed through possibilities. Therefore, you have the actuality, which is the original thought, and then its opposite allows for multiple experiences to be derived from it.

One movement of thought creates an opposite to exist, with possibilities of other examples of that movement in line with the original thought. This can be viewed through an individual experience, or through the complexity of all life everywhere.

Original thought created one movement of life. Through the opposite being accessed, then multiple programs and dimensions were created. Hence, one exact movement for creation is divided up into opposite values of itself. See it as one program of life. One actuality of how creation is programmed to exist. It is best viewed as the centre point of a wheel, having another 7 examples of itself through multiple wheels around the centre point of the original program. Therefore, 8 programs in total. The original program having an opposite of itself through 7 examples of possibilities.

However, there is also a third formula. This formula exists within the "core" of the original program. It contains the inversion formula to obliterate all thought and memory that is no longer required. It seeks out all obsolete codings of life that are no longer required within the program of that particular dimension. These three formulas can be related to as the "trinity" aspect of life. A tri-level response to all life within the building blocks of creation of that particular sector of space.

Initiates are not sent to the original program at all, but are sanctioned into the lower dimensions of time and space. This is due to the point of impact spoken of earlier. Their experience is to commandeer all opposite responses within each program into one dimensional response.

This being the case, then the power of the "real" is able to enter, allowing for the total remembering to take place. The initiate is then allocated a "new" program within the old, so as to divert all old coding within their human embodiment into a related power range for the "real" to be maintained consciously.

This, in itself, is difficult indeed. However, in line with what the initiate has come to experience, the opportunity to realise the power range of the "real" within the past is examined. The similarity of exchange from one program to another is often the cause of failure for many initiates who are immersed in self doubt, and thus are only able to have a proportional response instead of the full response needed to move away from a particular circumstance and/or environment.

The initiate who has been shielded from an actual movement of uncovering the purpose to their journey, are often filled with a sense of non-purpose within their life. Their thoughts and actions denote a need to be involved in humanitarian issues, so as to derive a sense of fulfilment in helping others. This may sound rather trite in itself. However, it certainly offers the initiate an opportunity to understand the divisional aspect of life within the Lower Worlds whilst awaiting the call to awaken.

Multiple programs are not able to be fully understood whilst occupying a human consciousness, because of the complexity of these programs holding a language barrier to the conscious recognition of their true worth. Initiates, therefore, are only able to rely on their sensory perception, rather than their conscious recognition of what these programs hold.

For many initiates their inner feelings, rather than their outer understanding, is put to a powerful test. Those who have resisted the outer life as being their power point of existence will be at an advantage, whilst those who have grown used to the matter body within the world of substance, will have a great deal of difficulty in releasing their outer world for their inner remembering.

Each dimension holds all other dimensions within it. A composite of programs, all occupying the same space, but resonating within a different ratio of sound. You can liken it to one room that holds multiple other rooms within it. Each room occupying that particular frequency enables it to appear as if it was a single room in itself.

However, each room, when viewed as a unit of space with multiple waves of sound, is recognised as one room only. One single response to a multi-dimensional sector of space. The inhabitants of the Lower Worlds find it difficult to perceive this very fact. They are reluctant to perceive divisional thought, let alone divisional space, which, of course, is one and the same.

The five senses within the framework of human life upon the Planet Earth offers a limited range of awareness. In fact, it is a primitive evolutionary concept that eliminates any factor that does not encompass these five senses. Unbeknown to these inhabitants, they have eight senses, not five. The other three senses have been subdued through the human evolution chain because of the dissent between the negative and positive forces of energy that exist within the Lower Worlds.

The structure of life within these Worlds offers little to the initiates who awaken to the "real". However, the opportunity to locate the three "missing" senses is offered, so as to assist them upon their journey. These senses swing into action once the power of the "real" has entered the total consciousness of the human embodiment.

The power point of these senses are located within the cellular memory bank that bypasses the central nervous system via the brain. They are relayed through a bypass mechanism through the higher energy bodies, rather than through the human energy bodies. The higher energy body is fully functional once the "point of impact" is achieved, and one dimensional response is ascertained for the "real" to enter. The energy of the "real" is the adjudicator for the "missing" three senses to be activated. When this occurs, the next chapter to the initiate's journey begins.

The parallel aspect of divisional dimensions is interesting indeed when researching the need to find the "missing" three senses. In line with the story of life and the participants within it, the power base behind the progression through the Lower Worlds is difficult indeed with only the 5 senses to rely upon.

However, the initiate is always within reach of locating these three senses, for the story of life is only the illusionary aspect of existence. The "real" is the mainstay for the movement within the dimensions, highlighting the factor of 7 levels, with the 8th being the final dimension required for the elimination of all obsolete coding.

The criteria for an on-going movement through all dimensions relies heavily upon the point of impact being accessible. For the sub-frame of consciousness to embrace the need to exist only within one response upon each dimension is paramount indeed, in order to implement the "real" into one's full conscious awareness.

The 7 levels of existence are composed of layers of thought. Each layer being a sub-division of that level. In fact, there are 7 layers, being the composite of that level. You could view it as being 7 layers of awareness within one dimensional thought.

Each dimension holds the opportunity for multiple possibilities to occur. Each possibility holds a number of outcomes, relegated to the ratio of sound within that particular dimension. For example, one dimension offers the opportunity for an extensive number of outcomes to occur, whilst another dimension only offers a more minimal number of outcomes. Therefore, each dimension holds its own power ratio of thought. Each action holds the capacity to have a multiple of re-actions, but not beyond the number allocated to the power ratio of that particular dimension or program.

The key to the point of impact is to align oneself to limiting the number of responses to a particular issue. In other words, to not fragment one's thought beyond the need to become aware that all thoughts originate from one thought. The one thought has to be the prime objective for any initiate to maintain its focus upon, in order to return back into the one response, for the return "home" to begin.

Singularity denotes the proportion of essence away from the power point of itself. In order to experience the Lower Worlds within the entirety of the experience to be had, one has to maintain a bond between the world of illusion and the reality aspect of the initiate's journey.

Whilst illusion is the mainstay of one's reality, then the need to become aware of what lies beyond one's reality is stifled through the realisation that life, being the reality aspect of awareness, holds all thought necessary for the advancement towards a greater understanding, but still of the same thought.

Thought within illusion holds a rotating aspect of itself, with all thought and action being cyclic. New thought is inundated with old thought, in order to promote the inaccurate measurement of development and progression. In order to recognise this acknowledgement as being factual, then you need to look within memory, with memory holding the key to the rotation of all thought.

Memory is the provider for the fuel to ignite old thought whilst re-living itself through fragments of truth, instead of the exact acknowledgement of all thought and action that occurred. For thought holds to itself nothing but an injunction to provide inaccurate data through time.

So, when we look at dimensional thought being brought into one response, then the initiate needs to rely upon the inner memory instead of believing the image of thought through time. The product of imagery does little to assist in understanding the point of impact. For through the multiple levels of awareness comes a joint formation of thought that must be perceived as being one thought only having possibilities, but not actualities occurring.

The sum total of programs within the range of the past provides the initiates with a complexity that they can ill afford. For the complexity of memory that is no longer needed to be drawn upon will stifle the main point of remembering of what the journey is all about.

There is always a side line to the basis of truth, in that truth is formatted with aspects of itself to be identified in many, many ways. Not detracting from the truth, but instead viewing it as by-products to be evaluated within the desired circumstance, so as to arrive at the destination of acknowledgement intact.

The object of relativity within the many dimensions of thought is through a minor power grid that defines the relationship of awareness to the many and varied opportunities, so as to characterize its definition of truth. Hence, the one dimensional relationship to all levels of awareness is heeded when there is no need to define truth at all, but instead know that truth is the fallacy of the programs in order to have a relativity factor to view through. This being the case, it allows for the many dimensions to exist.

However, if only one program of thought is available, then all other programs cease to be because relativity is no longer viable through the vantage of viewing the "no-truth" within all thought.

Imagery and truth are really one and the same, all having aspects of thought, to retain the current perception that is required to exist for the circumstance of the initiate to be maintained whilst within the Lower Worlds.

The policy of persistence is required to create the many examples of life experience to be had. This is to be done without losing the inner awareness of the purpose to the journey. Thus the relationship to the singular aspect of life is paramount to the success or non-success of the journey.

All thought is paramount to the existence of the time line and its rotation of experiences to be had. So within the recognition that created thought does not exist, except to re-create it, then the initiate is at a loss as to how to manifest a "correction" to that thought, so as to impart the "new".

Within the multiple time-lines through the linear concept, each dimension or program exists within a different ratio of time. Each program holds a different sound, which has a variance of either 3, 4 or 5 (+ or -):1. The comparative factor of 1 being, of course, the point of your reference within the 8th realm of existence.

There is a rotating value of sound within a number of grids that relate to each program. Each grid holds the value of life to which that particular program is framed towards. For each program has a reactive aspect that contains multiple opportunities to allow the measurement of sound to be encased with a fractional response rather than through the power range of an exact response.

To this end, this sounds indeed, complex, and for the uninitiated it is. However, to one who is able to master the formula of reasoning through the memory of the initiate, then complexity turns into simplicity itself.

There is always a framework of division between aspects of life upon each dimensional value of experience. This division, as was spoken of before, operates within a variable sound range through regulating the point of impact into one main note or sound that resonates only to the program monitor involved. Now I am really becoming complex to those who have not as yet mastered remembering. And so, I will offer to you the simple answer through your human conscious recall, so as to register a greater awakening to what you already know, but have forgotten, or indeed, chosen to forget.

There is a Master Coding formula that operates through multiple grids. These grids operate multiple energy beams that circulate the complete spectrum of sound through a cycle. That cycle is composed of many thoughts that have long been discarded. This is because it is referred to as the "old program" rather than the original program.

Throughout each frame of existence, lies many corridors, or entry points into sub space. Sub space being the counterpart of space itself. It could be likened to an extension to space, but not of the space at all. It is populated by sub species rather than the structure of species that is contained within the program of the "real" space.

To put it simply, means that sub space is the holding place for life forms that have not reached their true potential, and could be seen or acknowledged as "off- shoots" from the programming system mentioned earlier, whereby rotating grids offer many opportunities to complete the cycle of life.

Sub-space does not allow the completion to occur, but instead shows the reverse in action. Species revert back to the beginning of their cycle, but never to the end. It could be likened to a movement that never reaches its true potential, but instead stops before it discovers it's true identity.

Linear time does not exist there, but instead it is recorded as limited movement towards the end, but always reverting back to the beginning again. Therefore, the beginning to the end is never experienced.

The harmonics of sound offer little respite to the dwellers within the sub worlds, for they are oblivious of the power range of sounds that would offer to them an understanding for the purpose of life. They are constantly being "co- created" with other life forms, depending upon the alteration required to reimburse the requirement of those needing an outcome of an energy formula to fit their needs.

The lesser is always seen as an abstract quality in order to reach the greater. The greater being the ultimate opportunity for many to instil their own power grid into many sectors of space. For within their "greater", lies the point of impact of bringing so many possibilities into just a few.

There is a resistance within the sub worlds towards keeping the original thought operational. Therefore, interference with many programming formulas provides the opportunity to never allow what is "original" to return back into itself. Hence, the power range of the duplication process is protected, and multiple life forms are reconstructed over and over again, in order to promote this point.

To use the term "evolution" is to offer a beginning and an ending. To provide opportunities for the expansion of awareness of a life form towards its recognition of its total capacity to go beyond itself into a new example. However, with the interference by those who use their own power base to obstruct this process, it is then referred to as the Duplicate World, which is far removed from the Original Plan. The Duplicate being, of course, taking an imprint of the Original and transforming it into a different example altogether. When you look at the term "duplication' you would expect that a desired result would occur.

Taking the Original as the forerunner to offer up an opportunity to construct an exact from it, and insert differing possibilities, so that it finally moves away from its first intent and purpose from its Original state towards a completely different set of opportunities altogether. However, an Original is something that cannot be duplicated at all. I will give to you an example:

"A thought that is duplicated by another is always coloured by another's thought. You therefore cannot have two thoughts the same. For the first thought is always the base for other thoughts to come from. Any other thought, even though it is duplicated, is always immersed in another's interpretation of that thought".

This may sound complex in itself, but it is not. To understand thought as being the provider for other thoughts is the entrance to understanding what I am saying. From the Original provider of the thought comes the Original thought. To duplicate that thought by anyone or any other means of creativity is to completely alter that thought through the journey to which they are currently upon.

This works in both the lesser and the greater. To the human, it comes from the transfer of another's thought into the memory bank of all of their thoughts. Then the thought that they have duplicated into their attitude or their response then becomes, not the original at all, but a duplication thereof. Thus being completely changed through all other thoughts that they hold within them.

Evolution is the construction of multiple opportunities that infiltrate the program of the mind. The Higher Mind, of course, being the Original movement for the beginning of the cycle of evolution and the ending, so that the next opportunity can begin. All life forms have a cycle of evolution so that a progression can take place. That is the Original thought.

The Duplication being, of course, an altered version that can never have a beginning and an ending, but instead has a cycle of a never-ending revolution of thought that has no progression at all. Therefore, the Duplicate World is simply a World that is composed of a constant revolution of multiple opportunities, being divided and sub-divided over and over again.

Now, let us speak about a co-host. What is a co-host, and what connection does it have to the Duplicate World that has been spoken of? Firstly, you have to remind yourself that there are multiple responses to a program. A program of course being the result of a thought that creation emits to ascertain an awareness factor on multiple levels of awareness. Each level of awareness believing in its own viability totally, oblivious to itself existing upon other dimensions. Multiple programs co-existing together, unaware that others exist.

Each program is divided up into 7 sub-frames of existence. These sub-frames are multi-layered thought patterns that enable the initiate to relate to the imprint value of memory that is the mainstay of all relativity of thought within each program.

This description then leads us into creating an opportunity to relay what a co-host actually is. It is a parasite factor that draws from what has already been, to empower itself, rather than create anything that is new. It draws from the imprint factor of memory to re-enforce itself as a separate identity away from the original thought.

You could liken each program as having a host (not to be confused with a co-host) to offer the opportunity for growth via multiple possibilities through the 7 sub-frames of existence. Each program's host is called "a benefactor", which is the insertion of new thought, so as to allow a different relativity factor to occur.

Therefore, memory does not hold the cyclic rotation of thought to empower itself, so that the growth of awareness is negligible.

However, within the Duplicate World there are co-hosts, that have been created to defeat any awareness at all. These parasites are simply thought patterns to sabotage and eliminate any advancement of thought that would have been possible through a benefactor of new thought. Therefore, all that remains is simply the old program that has been run and re-run countless times, imprisoning all who remain within its structure of time/space.

The Original thought that created the programs encoded "a benefactor" within each program. This would allow for the awareness factor to be rotated into another opportunity with new thought being in place, to provide different possibilities to occur the next time it was run. However, with the sabotage factor of negating new thought with co-hosts, then the rotation factor within each program empowers the past thought, rather than offering to it another thought to create a different awareness factor.

After being re-run over and over again, the Original thought has been completely annihilated by the co-hosts. Each program can now be viewed as being a power point of duplicated memory, which is far removed from the Original memory. Nothing within these programs can ever leave the cycle of destructive and inaccurate memory that they contain.

There is no chance of advancement and growth, for the co- hosts within the Duplicate World have forced all who live within these programs to lose sight of new thought and new action. The ability to live without the inaccuracy of memory is not possible. Therefore, through this understanding, an initiate is faced with either recognising the "real" within their energy structure of light, or face the illusion of memory within the energy structure of their life.

The circumstances that have been chosen to formulate the pattern of one's life is formulated from the residue of experiences pertaining to programs that have not been fully recognised by the initiate. The structure of memory is always divisible into what is known and what is unknown, and in this regard lies the circumstances to one's inheritance and indeed, one's memory of their very purpose within existence.

There is an overview of circumstances within each action that one takes. To view the factual of the plan of existence is to view the point where existence originated from. This cannot be done through the misrepresentation of memory via the lesser within one's perception of memory. For memory holds multiple circuits of profound and exact power ranges that need to be regarded as the point of observation through which one should live through.

For example, each program has within it a central point of observation. This central point is the calendar to which time is derived from. It holds the essence of light and the essence of darkness that brings the program its rightful component of experience for all life to move through. This central core is a direct link-up with another central core within another program, and so on. As each program explodes its power range outward, and not inward as most believe, then the power point of observation becomes valid within each opportunity that each possibility brings.

The purpose of memory is to validate each action. Remember that. Memory is the recording system of thought, and as each thought is expressed through action or non- action, then the recording of that thought highlights the program to which one belongs to. Each program has a central core, to which was spoken of earlier, but the central core also holds the main formula for existence. Within the mainstream data bank of each program, memory becomes the inheritance for all life to draw from. thereby thought being the prime producer of maintaining the program's directive.

The structure of memory within each program differs, because each central core provides a different power point than another. The sound within the central core delivers outwardly the necessary power range to which all thought will derive from. Thus, thought will be so variable as each program is seen and understood by the initiate.

The main program can be viewed as being the entire range of all programs into one point, which of course is referred to as "the point of impact". All thought within each program offering the initiate the option to journey through the entire spectrum of sound as one main sound, or to use each program as one's inheritance, thus belonging not to the journey of the initiate, but to the journey of the Lower World inhabitant.

Each initiate is offered up the opportunity to journey through each program as a means to understanding the Lower Worlds, but not to belong to the ideology of it at all. Unfortunately, the purpose of initiating the sound so that "the point of impact" can be acknowledged by the initiate often goes unnoticed, and the result of denying the reason for one's journey is the closing of the door to the remembrance of what one truly is. When this occurs, then the initiate is on their own within the denseness of a particular program, unable to remember the journey at all.

When the sound is sent out, it is done through the central core, so that a "new" power range can permeate outwardly into each program. Each initiate is responsible for the outcome of their response. The journey thus far has included a range of options that the initiate has to take into consideration in order to remember the purpose of the journey.

Within the remembrance of the intent, comes the need to remember what is "real" rather than embracing the forgetfulness through the power point of singularity.

The simple within the intent often becomes the complex within the sound of the past. The tri-level aspect of life is re-arranged when the parity chambers are reversed. The sound of "all" is immersed with the self-doubt of even wanting to view that life is but only a small aspect of remembrance through the awakening of the totality of what one really is.

The fact of the matter is clearly defined when the object of the "intent" undergoes a metamorphose and is replaced by sheer self-indulgence of what can be fulfilling, rather than the object of recognising the sound of what the "intent" is to reveal. This statement is not a matter of conjecture at all, but is to clearly outline the difficulty that is faced by all who do not wish to remember, but rather wish to forget.

Let us talk about "intent". What is the intent within the journey, and how can it be realised? A main point to be considered is the need to empower the intent rather than release the power within the intent. The statuary component within this realisation shows itself through many ways:

- Memory is both the annihilator and the provider of remembering.
- It is the tool to either observe or deny the intent.
- It is the reference point to begin or end one's journey.
- The emphasis on the "intent" will define whether the purpose of the journey can be validated or not.

The challenge of life is surely through one's need to permit the truth to be entered into.

Within the "intent" aspect of recognising the truth within all thought and all action, the need to permit the opening up of new perimeters of thought is experienced.

Through the framework of thought lies the recognition of sound. Sound being, of course, the power within the thought that allows the thought to begin and end. The customary action that accompanies that thought is often defined as the truth within the thought. However, that is not accurate.

The intent within an action is not always viewed, for within the thought lies the foundation of intent. However, the action that is connected to that thought may be totally different than the thought itself. Thought needing another thought to survive. There can never be a single thought that is not attached to another thought. The process of thought through one's intent is only recognised by another thought. This needs an explanation:

The Original thought that created life is composed of fragments of itself, so as to validate itself. Thought is a composite of all thought. It can never be realised through one single thought, for it needs all thought to show itself to itself. Intent is the operating factor of releasing thought back into itself, so as to demonstrate the movement of thought. However, when thought does not deliver the intent, for the intent has become separate from the thought, then deceit is imminent. A breakaway pattern of thought has been established, for the intent does not justify the thought through action. In this simple statement, therein lies the complexity of life. What is programmed through intent to be experienced and explored, does not always eventuate.

The program of one's inheritance is seen as the viewing station of life. It is the point whereby the opportunity to view what was, is clearly defined through the "experience" through memory, rather than through memory only. This fact is clearly reinforced when understanding that the human vantage point of viewing the past is via a powerful resonance of memory that the inheritance has encountered.

This of course differs from the awareness factor of memory via thought, or to put it simply .. via the collective consciousness of all thought.

There is always a simple answer to the question of truth. Truth always lies. That is the simplicity within the answer. The complexity is, of course, still to be defined into a powerful awareness that is both through the observer and the observed. The obstinate need to not view oneself is because of the need to always view others first. The observer wishes to observe what is presented through their current perspective of truth. However, when the observer is faced with the observation point of what is defined as "truth", then the matter of truth becomes one's need to define it according to the point of observation through the inheritance factor of memory.

Truth is always a definition of observation, rather than a point of actuality. It is the result of an action, rather than the actual action itself. Therefore, the action is never regarded as the "truth" but instead the result of the action becomes the point of observation for truth to be defined from. The image of what is regarded as the truth, is usually the point of observation to observe the next truth, and so on. With this in mind, then one needs to consider where the "original" truth began and ended.

The way-station of thought is through the boundary of observation. For when one observes, then one surely has to become aware of the boundaries placed on the observation factor of defining truth. For to totally view the truth is surely to firstly define one's observation of truth through the memory of what truth is. An observation of truth may be viewed through the following simple example:

"There is a large tree that has grown so tall that it is blocking out the sunlight to the small plants below, and if they do not receive the light, then they will die.

The tree, however, is home to many, many species of birds who use the upper branches as a haven for their young ones, to keep them far away from any predators that might cause danger to their young.

Is the tree too tall or not? That is the point of observation. What is the truth? Of course, it depends upon who the observer is, as to the definition of truth. The small plants will die so that the young birds may live. Or perhaps the tree should die, so that the plants may live and the birds will have to choose another place to have their young. And so it goes on, and on and on".

Truth is a complete fallacy and should be seen as such. It is the observation point of one's current perception but is not, and should not be viewed as the truth, but rather as an observation of a current perception of truth. An initiate is faced with many and varied experiences that will present many truths that hold nothing but the hope that they are the truth. For to believe in someone or something is to place upon them the burden of always being the truth for your observation to be based upon.

The most obvious question that must be asked .. "What governs the Lower Worlds?" When this question is asked, then the initiate is viewing from beyond the boundary of belonging to the falsity of human life, and instead is drawn towards understanding the power that governs that life.

The purpose to life is often questioned by many whom have their own personal power base threaded through the answer. The question and answer must match, equal to the enquirer. I will explain: The deliverer of the message of life is through the human language that is governed by the past. The past has served many by giving them the power from the truth to deliver to others.

Religion has its power base solely upon the past. All who deliver the truth of the past are revered as being the saviours of the future. The past and future have to be in line with each other, so that the deliverer may be empowered through the title of "deliverer".

The deliverer being the self-imposed example of truth by joining the past and the future together. Many prophets have been either condemned or revered simply by viewing the future, relative to the needs of those to whom it was intended. To intimate that the future will be free of the power of the now was to entice fear and retribution. However, if the future was a continuation of the current time, equal to the needs of those to whom the prophecy was given, then the prophet was given a hero's welcome.

The power point to life has always been held in so few hands, so that the many can be manipulated through fear of not being in control of the outcome of life. Therefore, if one is not responsible for one's life, then who or what is? This fallacy then becomes operational by drawing past references into the future, with the now being the bridge to bring them altogether.

I have spoken of the falsity of human life and the purpose thereof. The governing factor of humanity is, in fact, humanity. However, beyond humanity and the fallacy to which it follows, through religious dogma, the true power that controls the Lower Worlds can be revealed.

What is the purpose to life? Does life have a purpose, or is it an enigma, waiting to be revealed by those to whom can gain no benefit at all from the answer or answers. When there is no benefit to the enquirer as to the answer, then there is an open-ness to discovery.

The need to ask this question is as important as the answer to be found. For in needing to know the purpose of life, the need to have the answer is equal to one's intent.

The intent will discover the answer, rather than the need to know. For one only locates an answer to a question equal to their expectation of the answer given and the agreement thereof of the answer itself. The purpose of life equals the purpose of enquiry. To believe in the answer before the question arises is to delay the need to know. However, when the intent is equal to the question, which is equal to the outcome or the answer, then one is totally unopposed to finding the answer after all.

Is there a controlling factor to life? What is the purpose for the beginning and the ending of life? Is the self, the "me" the "you" an opportunity ready to begin, or is it the ending of the cycle of opportunity that needs to be recognised? Is humanity the power broker to life, self-creating, or being created?

The observation factor of viewing life is to firstly view the intent for life to begin and end. When viewing the intent with the power of one's own intent, then together a union begins, and the revelation of life begins to unfold. There was never a time when life was not, and within that statement lies the uncovering to the understanding of life.

When one views life, then one views a concept of life, but not life at all. For within the word "life" therein lies a powerful intent and purpose for the revelation to begin. Life is a multi- faceted arrangement of sound. Sound being the conductor and distributor of thought. Thought having the power to divide itself over and over again into many examples to connect to the opportunity of experience.

Each experience is the off-shoot of thought. Each thought being the divisible sum of sound. Sound, of course, being clearly defined through multi-facets of itself so that the Original thought may be viewed and experienced through many aspects of itself. Thus the point of reference being the faceted power point to which all come from and all return.

When viewing the purpose for life to begin and end, as mentioned before, one needs to view the intent firstly of needing to know, rather than the curiosity factor of knowledge. For knowledge is often categorised into components of acceptability.

Each component has been carefully analysed and tested, so that the truth may be ascertained, rather than the falsehood of theory that has failed the test through past reference of knowledge.

The simple answer to the purpose of life, is that life just "is". And when the "is" is examined, rather than "life", then this leads to a whole outpouring of opportunity to go beyond one's concept of theory and knowledge. Let us firstly view life as a concept, rather than what is real. That concept is the past measurement through memory of what life represents. All life has a blueprint. That blueprint is from the centre most point of observation pertaining to its structure to sustain itself within a certain environment. Environment is linked to the chain of life. Life is linked to the need to experience the environment. Life cannot be seen solely as the experience itself, but is the forerunner to the reason for its existence.

Within existence lies the foundation of experience to begin and end. In between the beginning and the ending, the point of observation occurs as to whether life can be sustained or not. Whilst life is seen as the cumulative example of which to follow, then surely one does not estimate the purpose within the existence, ascertaining whether the existence has a beginning or not.

The complexity within these statements highlights the importance to withstand the directive of enquiry. Not into the need to understand the very purpose of life, so that it can be seen as a prelude to a greater understanding of life, but instead it should be viewed as the "real and true example" to follow to reveal what life truly "is".

Substance plays a part in unfolding the tomorrows for life to continue, with substance being the key role player in ascertaining where one belongs in the story of creation, within the revelation of what life beholds. For within the core of all memory that justifies the existence of life, lies the answer to which all seek, but all do not wish to find lest they find the answer they are not seeking. There is no judgement when locating the need to understand what the existence factor of the "me and you" means. When the result of life looks for the purpose to its life, then there is a means test firstly of wanting to locate a truth that befits the measurement of one's worth.

Singularity is not life. That is a fact. It is only a by-product of what is possible. Through that possibility, lies the forerunner of becoming aware of what singularity could become. However, the single aspect through the human endeavour to reach into the mysteries of creation leaves a large gaping hole in the truth odyssey for existence to be explained.

To locate the purpose of something is to reach into the limitation of needing to find it, and we have already spoken of this, in part. However, in reaching into the full contingency of what life truly "is", then one has to determine firstly as to whether one is ready to know or not.

There is no secret to life. It is an open door to all who wish to enter. It holds only what one will understand without the prejudice of needing to know. It fulfils everything and nothing within the entirety of its choice of maintaining the truth through the intent of who has entered. There is no justification within life, for life is the fundamental player to operate the vast network of opportunities for the power of the Original thought to begin and end through the cycle of opportunity that one calls "life".

The initiate, when confronting the personal deity of life, often misjudges their own powerful ability to not wanting to know, rather than see it as a point of observation to move through.

That brings us to look firstly at the facts of illusion within the understanding of life. Illusion is the result of reality taking a break from revealing itself.

An unusual statement, and yet a very powerful one when one is looking to enter into the power of the intent of revealing the "is" of life.

What is real about life? Another question, with another answer awaiting. However, when this question follows on from the understanding that life is a paradox, then we are ready to begin to unravel and reveal the true purpose of life itself.

Chapter 2

Gently, I awoke to find you there. Looking down upon me with those eyes. Eyes that were of the deepest blue, and yet held the memory of all that ever was and all that "is".

"Is it over?" I asked. "Is it finally over?" His words were quiet when he said "no, it is not over, but it is finally beginning".

Those few words were to reveal the greatest story that was never written. It is the story of my life. And who am I? Well, I am someone who doesn't really exist, except within the character that has been chosen to share this story with you.

I am the reflection of the past and the future, and within the now is where you will find me. I have been created, so the story of life can be told within the human language of expression.

Your question is, of course, directed to the one with the eyes that were of the deepest blue. To whom or what am I referring? Why it is my true identity .. the "real" me. The part of me that knows the way the journey of life needs to go. Through the character that I am, I would become hopelessly lost, for the life that I believed that I belonged to finished that day .. and the "real" me emerged so that the beginning could indeed begin.

All stories start at the beginning .. and this story is certainly no exception. A beginning has to have a reason for existence, so that the storyline will follow the natural course to provide an opportunity for the reason to show itself. Where there is a beginning, there must also be an ending. And what is an ending? But an opportunity for it all to begin again! Is this a paradox? Yes it is, but then so is life.

Welcome to the beginning ....

I took my place within the Chamber and joined all who had come to listen to the advocate of the Higher Council. There was a stillness all around that permeated through the entire Chamber. Within this stillness, there was a sense of peace. A powerful antidote that allowed for all who were present to draw from the silence what they required, so as to be at one with their inner thoughts.

A powerful reminder of one's true identity is always found through the silence, and not through the many images that favour the journey through many and varied realms that I have ventured within. For one's true identity holds the totality of experiences from many into the one.

A single mind offers little to the progression of the "one". For the "one" is the complete content of all lives that have been lived, and all experiences that have been undergone. The fabric of one's destiny is only a single thread to be woven into the complete understanding of what the "one" represents, and to be standing here within this Chamber, offered to me the opportunity to listen to a singular "being" that was speaking on behalf of so many.

The silence became more powerfully effective as the moment drew near to when the advocate would appear before us, for within the silence all is felt and all is known. Time has no definition here and sound is not required, for the advocate does not use language to convey the message from the Council, but instead uses a mind to mind meld, that allows each one to become a part of the message to be given.

The directive was given .. the advocate had arrived. All were required to be seated, ready to listen inwardly to what needed to be conveyed. I felt anticipation rise up within me. Perhaps it was on this day that a new assignment would be forthcoming. I felt ready to meet the challenge.

A single sound was sent out, and within that sound all minds came into "one". The advocate spoke to the "one", and all individual thought through the power of differing experiences was immediately over-ridden by the "one" true sound that drew all into the collectiveness of the experience.

The advocate stood before us, dressed in a garment of light that shone throughout the Chamber upon that day, and within that light the sound of the "one" was heard by all.

"I have come unto you all, so that you may understand the directive of the High Council of which I represent upon this day. There is dissension within the Lower Worlds of the past. Many initiates have not returned home, and we fear the worst. The sound of the few that have returned home have spoken of travellers dressed in garb that have created many images to re-direct them into many places that were not a part of their journey.

Some were seen to succumb to the advances of these travellers, believing that they could take a quicker route through the Lower Kingdoms, in order to return home. However, they were not heard of again. Many are believed to be within the sub-worlds of the Lower Heavens, and this being the case, then we need to create a dream whereby they can be reached.

All who are here upon this day are required to enter the Dream Chamber, so as to enter into the Lower Worlds once again. Instructions will be given to you upon entering. We thank you."

As he left the Chamber, the power of the "one" was withdrawn, and I was left to my own thoughts. My next assignment had been given to me. It would not be easy, but I had trained many of those initiates, and I knew I could help.

The Dream Chamber has long been regarded as the pinnacle of one's entry into other Worlds, whereby entry through the usual method of "birthing" was denied to all who sought permission to enter these Worlds. It allowed for the power of experience to be had through multiple receptor channels that harmonised with the Main Chamber of remembrance, so that at all times the awareness factor of what one truly is can never be over-ridden by the images found within the Worlds to which one has entered.

The time variance was matched to permit an experience through a time ratio befitting the opportunity. In other words, the Dream was played out through a moment in the Dream Chamber to match multiple years or rotations in the World just entered.

One moment is viewed as a flash of experience that is rolled out into a time management system, relevant to the World that is to be entered. Time therefore is stretched out accordingly. The adjustment from the point of entry via the Dream Chamber has to be carefully aligned with one's structure of thought, for to hasten the entry from the collective world of light into the Lower Worlds of matter, would create undue stress on the energy structure of one's entire being.

The Dream is matched exactly to the co-ordinates of the time/space imprint that is required to be experienced, and at no time is there ever a variance so as to divert the Dream through and into multiple Dreams. This rule is always applied to the main point of entry into other Worlds, so that whoever enters the Dream Chamber are always aware that only one Dream has been entered into, and if any other Dream becomes one's reality, then the illusion factor exists.

Time is the measurement of experience equal to the ratio of energy of where one has been sent. This seems to be a paradox in itself, for in measuring time there needs to be a point of reference in which to refer to. Whilst one is within time, then the reference point is null and void, except through the memory of what it is not. When entering a Dream Chamber, time is only understood by the "x" factor of reference. I will explain:

"x" is an unknown factor unless it has a relativity aspect of reference. For example, an action has a relativity factor equal to the time left after the experience, but not before. Time therefore is what remains after the event, rather than before the event occurred. The event or action occupies the sum total of space equal to the ratio of energy that still remains. With this in mind, then the relationship between time and no-time can be more clearly defined.

When time is viewed as a linear movement, then this very movement needs to have a relativity factor to the next action or event. However, if time was viewed differently, through multiple insertions via differing programs and possibilities, then time would be seen as a revolving example, rather than a consecutive factor.

Memory is time. Each memory operates on a frequency base that offers an image of the event rather than the exact event. Memory therefore is either viewed with an elongated or restricted reference point, but the content of time of the actual event is not accurately registered. For after the event, the point of reference has been altered by constant images of other memories. This example simply illustrates that time is an inaccurate measurement of an event.

The Dream Chamber reflects one into the Lower Worlds, not through the linear "time" reference point, but instead through the Inner Chamber that rotates them through differing programs and possibilities. Time, as was stated before, ceases to be a measurement but instead becomes the factor whereby a "new" dream can be inserted. It depends upon where one is viewing from as to whether this paradox can be understood. From the image of time difficulty arises to incorporate a non-measurement into a system of constant measurement.

To summarise, the need to reflect into time creates an altered relationship to the experiences that will be encountered. Whilst within time the duration or measurement factor of the experiences are viewed through the linear rather than the actual. The linear being the point of observation that the physical embodiment occupies within a program. Hence, the duration factor within the illusionary linear time is an elongated experience rather than a factual one.

Therefore, one moment within the Dream Chamber equals many illusionary Earth years.

The power to preserve the memory of what one is, as opposed to the memory of what one inherits, is the greatest obstacle to the reflection. The difficulty lies in integrating the reflective energy into the inherited embodiment within the specific time/space continuum.

The Inner Chamber holds many power ranges that are activated at various intervals. It resonates on a multi-band sound frequency, otherwise known as a multiple coding system, which over-rides all previous coding formulas of old programs. In turn, this then allows for "new" inserts to be placed within a program or programs, creating new possibilities for the transference of initiates from old programs into the "new" program.

The emergence from no-time into time is a powerful experience indeed for the initiate who desires to understand the singularity aspect of light. For within this journey lies the promise of re-living the sound of long ago, within the limited world of the past. However, for those who will enter the Dream Chamber, this experience is far from being regarded as a journey full of opportunity, but instead is regarded as an experience that need not happen, but for that which has incurred for it to be so. The Dream Chamber holds remnants of all programs that have long since been eradicated. Within it lies the principle element of the initial blueprint of light that came from the Greater Mind.

It can be viewed through one's image as being a portal within space that holds a vastness of all light as well as all life, everywhere. It synthesises a sound that upholds the Main Chamber to creation, so as to reflect the point of entry of they who have entered. It does not hold depth or width, but instead is composed of a multitude of rotating disks that oscillate constantly to the memory of the place to which one is being reflected. These disks are located within the centre most point of this Chamber, so as to provide the point of observation within the designated point in time and space.

There is a dual frequency within the Chamber. One frequency is located within the rotating disks, and the other becomes the constant, but in stasis, reference point. It could be described as holding the object or energy in place, whilst reflecting a duplicate of itself through the time and space point of reference. As described earlier, this takes but a few moments, but yet within the time/space aspect can be seen as many, many years or even aeons.

I took my place within the Dream Chamber and waited. A sound resonated through my whole being and I knew it had begun ...

Chapter 3

The young woman held her head in her hands and moaned .. "Please don't let me die. I think I am going to die!" A concerned man stood in front of her, reassuring her, telling her that her fears were unfounded. What she didn't know, was that her life was about to change drastically. I had just entered time .. the year was 1980, and she would be my host through the Lower Worlds.

It was obvious that the effect of my entry had created distress upon her physical demeanour, with her heart rate becoming erratic and her vital signs indicating a crisis at hand. Her fear confounded the difficulty, for she was unaware of what had just occurred, and at that stage, it was just as well. For there was much that had to be done before she could be confronted with the truth of that day.

The host that I had just entered had been created, rather than chosen. The journey that it had experienced through the cycle of reincarnation spanned over 275 years. A composite of 4 different personalities was drawn into one point, so as to present the best possible opportunity for my entry point into time/space. These 275 years were not consecutive, but instead were experienced through a broad spectrum of experience, encompassing different gender, culture and social values.

The totality of these lives created a more viable entry point, because of the de-regulation of permitting each previous life time as being a reference point for another, and so on. Instead, it was designated aspects of its previous lives, rather than the full regalia of memory. Thus bringing 4 sectional responses into one personality, rather than using a previous personality that had once lived. I will explain ..

Time is the recognition of a beginning and an end, and life is viewed through birth and death. A cyclic experience. All life consists of cyclic experiences, for what is created lives and then dies, to then live again. This is the natural law of evolution. All has been. All has died. All is again.

Time is the carrier of memory. All memory is relative to time. The entry into time opens up the Lower Worlds that once were, but are no more, except by triggering the time sequence again, so that they can be again. This is simple in itself when viewing it from no-time. However, when viewing it from time, then the simplicity becomes a frustrating analogy that shows no logic because of the reality clause to one's awareness through time.

The truth can never be seen through time, but if one could leave time and enter the timeless, then what has been spoken of would become very clear. How can it be explained to one who is in time that they no longer exist? To them, they do. They are real, very real, and all else beyond time does not exist. It is the paradox to the whole story. For the relativity factor exists here, and the difficulty in one's relationship to the truth lies within the boundary of time or no-time. Each has a different story to tell.

In this case, time was deregulated by composing a composite of memory into one point, rather than choosing someone who once did exist. To the uninitiated this would sound simple and indeed understandable. However, to those who are aware, then the consequence of this creation have numerable ramifications to the time-line of the past. Hence, the need to recognise "inserts" into programs as being the main contender for what is new to exist. Therefore, my host is an "insert" rather than an actuality, and with that in mind, I can now continue with the rest of the story.

My entry into time could be likened to an arrow, finding its mark and then continuing its journey through a configuration of multiple possibilities that had yet to take place in the new future, of course. Not what had been, but was yet to be, that had now been created as a "new program" of opportunity. For I had never entered through "this one" before, and so I could not exist within time unless a new program was devised to let it be so.

What had been would now run parallel to what will be through multiple possibilities to make it so. All I had to do was to influence my host to follow these possibilities, so that my journey did not end before it started. I was within all new possibilities, but the link-up to those possibilities was the deciding factor that would designate the success or failure of my entry into the Lower Worlds of time.

The fact still remains that until my entry into my host, she had a possible future held by a caretaker energy that would keep the entry point available until the time designated for my arrival. It should be noted that a temporary future is always afforded a host, so as to offer up another opportunity in the foreseeable future, if the connection point is unsuccessful.

Therefore, upon that day, the future changed. It no longer existed as such, but instead opened the door to a different outcome to her life, as well as many others, who were at that time oblivious that their future had also changed. The fabric of life had changed for so many, and the delicate task of altering the influence of the old future upon the now had begun.

Humanity dances to the tune of memory. Memory being the base for the beginning and ending of experience. What is not known, tried and explored is relegated a limited observation point for the adventurous, or some would say foolish. To influence a host is to impress that memory is to be placed aside, so that what is unknown can take its place. A difficult and intricate task that would take many years within time to accomplish.

Time could be likened to a major highway, running through all experiences. This highway is the main road that all take. What is known and what has been experienced by others, creates the pathway to enlightenment, or so they believe. Instead, it is the delusion of the traveller through time to believe this to be so.

Memory of life through time confines one to time. However, memory for the reason for life releases one from time into the timeless, where all is known and all is understood. There is a marked difference. For what is known does not need to be validated, for it just "is". Within this recognition, you will understand that my journey is fraught with uncertainty, and many who have attempted to enter a host within the Lower Worlds have met with failure, due simply to the power point of memory within their host.

However, I have been successful, or else this story would not have been written. I am here now, influencing my host in the Year 2000, who is now smiling at this introduction, and I know that she too, understands how difficult the journey has been.

My host is now integrated with many who have chosen the Dream Chamber to enter into the Lower Worlds, for many differing reasons. And so this story is devoted to all who now call her "their host". There will not be just one story to be told, but many. With each one sharing their experience, and their need to enter into the world of the past.

I will now commence the story, and as my story finishes, then another will take up the next part, and so on. The beginning of my story has been told, and the ending is still to be. However, my entry into the time and space of what is deemed to be the past has altered the course of my journey forever, and in fact for many others also.

My identity at this point shall not be disclosed, but as my story progresses, you will indeed understand the purpose to my intent. For to divulge who I am at the beginning of my story would not allow you the opportunity to see me clearly through each response that you will have. However you view me will depend upon who you really are.

The day that I entered time is the day that I entered Diane's life. The long process of interlinking her mind and mine began. It would take many years before she was even aware of me, but I was always there in the background of her mind, influencing her whenever I could so as to direct her towards a "new" direction and into a "new" program.

If I could at this point share a comparison with you. In comparing the Lower Worlds to where I come from, would be to imagine yourself within a place of peace, a place where all is tranquil and within order. Upon leaving that place you find yourself upon a busy street in one of the larger cities of your world. Each person's thoughts can be heard, intermingled with the noise of the traffic that uses that busy street.

Each person's thought is a thread to the collective consciousness of your World. Each thread makes up the loom of the collectiveness of all experience. Through all experience comes the acceptance of life within that point in time and space, for thought is the master of illusion, and the master is served by the repetitive need for the same thoughts. Through the need to keep experiencing the sameness, then life becomes the power broker of repetitive acceptance of all experience, and to go beyond this acceptance is to go beyond one's own acceptance within the mainstream of life.

Many initiates have asked about forgetfulness when one is within a host in the Lower Worlds. The answer is simple .. I do not experience forgetfulness. Instead I infuse my host's mind with the greater awareness that lies beyond her limited understanding. The host may choose to not accept what is "new", and therefore the host forgets .. I do not. Thought is very competitive in this World. It divides itself over and over again to find a way to alter its passage through each experience without ever being challenged. It over-rides other thoughts that get in its way, and it is often viewed as the power point of change, but yet I am still to see it. Belief, faith and trust seem to carry the greatest strength in this world. They ensure a collective resurgence towards the mastery of fear, whilst instilling fear. A strange World in which you live. A paradox in action.

Diane's World is your World. She lives within a program that has been carefully designed to create independent thought, through a collective acceptance. This program cultivates many and varied responses, especially within religion, culture and science. It is easily seen that a unit of thought can be managed more easily by the human consciousness, because of the need to belong to what is accepted by the many, rather than what is accepted by the few.

All in all, I have entered into a major highway of thought that is governed by a need to believe, rather than a need to question. Through that acknowledgement, I have entered into your World, so that I can experience what your World has to offer that stopped so many initiates from coming home. My host has assisted me in understanding so much over the time we have been together, for as her awareness grew of what was beyond this World of time, her mind blended with mine in search of answers.

From this point on, I shall refer to my host as H. Perhaps not a personal touch, but one that is more practical to the storyline. For my story is complex, and to relay it through the simplicity of human language will be difficult enough. My H is a product of life, and when I say that, I refer to what has been created, has been experienced and is now experiencing what has happened before. For my H is a product of time and of memory. Nothing new is experienced, for all has been, all is, and all will be. Time is being re-run over and over again, with multiple possibilities formulating the range of opportunities that have been taken before.

Humanity rarely looks at time as being composed of multiple strands, criss-crossing each opportunity to create a result. Each strand is a possibility of thought and action. It could be viewed as existing within multiple layered possibilities, all leading to the same result. A different version perhaps, but one that will lead you to the next opportunity to experience the multiple possibilities, and then back to the same result, and so on.

A difficult picture to paint, and yet so accurate that if you could view it totally, then you would understand that what you regard as "free will" is simply exercising your right to choose the sameness via multiple possibilities, over and over again.

I will explain: Time is the result of a program. The program will run over and over again, and you will end up at the same place regardless of what you choose. You will choose a different route, even have a different attitude, but unless you know that you are within a program that is being re-run over and over again, your choices will always take you to where you have been before. It is called the program of life. You are the character within it.

As a character, you have a role within the program. You are attached to the memory of time, and you are attached to the character that you are. You are unaware that you have the power to detach yourself from the character. You are locked into the program of your "self". Everything revolves around "you". Your character becomes so important to you, that nothing else exists. Unfortunately, that is the fact of the matter.

However gallantly you attempt to disengage yourself from the mainstream of life, and live an alternate existence, you are still a character within a program, but you just have a different expression within it. You are a product of life, just as my H is. Do not despair however, for in being totally aware of the program of life, is to understand its very design and how it has incorporated "you" within it.

You will need to be an observer of the program, rather than a continual participant that is unaware of how the program actually works. Thought is the active ingredient here. If you have thought that becomes aware, then you have the means to leave the program behind and move into a new program altogether that will show you the exit point into other realms of awareness.

You might ask at this point .. "But what thought do I need to become aware?" You firstly have to have the thought that nothing exists at all. Absolutely nothing. You are within a program of thought, but it is not the Original Thought. You have to start with the Original Thought that belongs to the "real" you. You are the Original Thought, not a character within a program. When you can know that, then you can begin to disengage yourself from the program of life, whilst still existing within it. You become the master of what you really are, observing what you are not. The mystery is then solved, and you become aware of your true identity.

There is a dual concept to the mastery of self. Within the understanding that you exist, but yet you do not, you are ready to unravel the very fabric of existence.

The common denominator to existence is consciousness. Within consciousness there is an overall acceptance of one's reality, and it is within the relativity factor of your need to control your reality that you can identify what you are not.

Control should be viewed as the ego in flight, moving through every aspect of one's life, shaping boundaries and constantly evaluating every action and thought that would lead to a greater awareness of one's own personal existence within the Greater Plan of Life. Through this limited response to life the ego remains the dominant factor, and one's true identity is overshadowed by the ego's constant need to validate itself through the sameness of its life. Change is for the future, and the now remains totally controlled by the reference to change, but not by any action at all.

With that in mind, we will now turn our attention to the basic structure of life, not the end result of it, but we need to focus upon the beginning, before "you" existed. For "you" are only in existence because of the thought that you would be. It is called the Original Thought, and it yields the power of all existence, whether it be in form or in a formless state of being.

"You" are here because of thought. The Original Thought contains the blueprint of all experience that needs to be. It has nothing to do with what has been, and at this point we need you to be totally aware of this fact. What has been is finished and should not be resurrected to be again. However, what is still to be should take the place of what has been, and so on. This is referred to as "the basic structure of life".

In the beginning before you existed, all existed. You are an aspect of what is termed "all". The "all" is the entirety of what you are .. before you began and before you ceased to be. This is simple in itself, and yet to the you who knows nothing else, the "all" is non-existent. And yet, to the "all", "you" are insignificant in the entirety of what it is.

The Original Thought is composed of light and sound. It is the common denominator of all existence everywhere, and it is the point of reference within this story, in order to explain what exists beyond the "you". For to not do so would illustrate and highlight your need to be the entirety of all that you ever were and all that you ever will be, and that line of thought would only validate the ego, and not the truth at all.

Have you ever asked yourself the question .. "Where was I before I existed?" Existence has to be formulated from something and not nothing. "You" came from existence, but you are not existence at all for "you" are a singular aspect of thought that has originated from the Original Thought.

That seems very impersonal to someone who is used to viewing life through the lens of personal endeavour, but no matter, for truth has to be upheld if the chain of response is to continue. Nothing can prevent the Original Thought from continuing to have its experience through "you". You exist within the time/space continuum of Planet Earth, as my H exists also within this state of being. However, what if this time/space was validated within the "has been" category, and not the "is still to be". That would make the now a very important part of your existence, wouldn't it?

Initiates were sent into the Lower Worlds, of which this time/space continuum is a part of, to view what "has been". Their test was to not become involved in what had failed, but instead to reach into the next chain of response of what is still to be. To remember what they are through what they are not. Unfortunately, upon entering the time/space of the Lower Worlds, many initiates become waylaid by their need to empower their new found singular thought pattern of humanity.

Many attempt to strengthen their thought, in order to gain access to their remembrance. However, unless the initiate can overcome their need to focus upon the self, their journey will become difficult indeed, and many will lose their way.

Within the Lower Worlds, a single life is seen as a gift from the creative force of all life, and within that gift a single thought exists. That thought is the sum total of what the "you" is comprised of. A singular unit of sound, governed by a chain of responses that reflect the thought of a singular existence, instead of the Original thought, which governs all thought.

The imprint of time, which is memory, is constructed of multiple bands of sound that have been formulated by singular thought, that has been empowered by cyclic repetition.

This thought becomes interlocked with itself, forming a vast network of sound that is constantly being accessed by humanity. This network of sound is also known as the fabric of life, and enables multiple possibilities to be accessed through the choice of thought, of which action is derived from. Whichever particular thought is chosen governs the next action within a possibility.

Within each possibility are multiple grid points. Each point is called a connector. This connector, by its namesake, connects and matches each thought to another thought, and so on, thus producing the possibility required to maintain that thought. One thought is divisible by its need to find an outcome, with that thought becoming the driving factor to move through life into the next opportunity.

There are many roads that lead to home. There are many possibilities that offer the initiate a way through time and the conscious awareness of singular thought. Many factors are involved in recognising the possibility that is best suited to the outcome, for within the new program the outcome eliminates further possibilities from occurring that originated from old programming procedures.

What is needed to be recognised at this point, is that for each possibility that aligns with old programs, there needs to be a connector of thought to a possibility within a new program. The new program will then demonstrate a pattern of observation firstly for the initiate, and then readily incorporate the next thought and action into an operative response. Through this operative response, comes the entire range of new possibilities to be connected to. Your question would be at this point .. "How can possibilities be in place, if it is a new program, whereby nothing has been experienced before?" There is a simple answer to this question...

A program is an exact opportunity to experience everything that needs to be experienced. It is a component of opportunity that is referred to as a "bypass" of old responses.

In itself, it is a complete experience covering many facets of opportunities that will shed light upon the pathway of each initiate. It spans the timeline, from the beginning to the end of all experience required within time by the initiate.

One's perspective of life alters as the new program is accessed. All old responses become nullified as the new program offers up different opportunities that require different responses. If an old response is given to a new opportunity or possibility, then the old program immediately becomes validated again. Nothing new can be accomplished when a need to hold onto old responses persists.

The new program is composed of sound waves that emit a constant frequency burst that aligns to the coding system of each initiate. It could be likened to a homing signal, sending out sound waves that trigger powerful memories of home. The awakening occurs, and each initiate is required to shed the fabric of life for their fabric of light.

The past has always called to each one, to rejoin the places and events that have governed each thought and action, but to do so would be to revert to the program of life. Therefore, the purpose to one's life, to the journey through life, is lost to the mainstream acceptance of the past. As we leave behind this awareness, and go instead to the paradox in action, which is, of course, the truth behind one's existence, through the program of the "self", then we shall find a different story altogether than the one that you have inherited.

Beyond time, life "is". Beyond your reference point of reality, life is in abundance. Your vision of life is coloured by what you believe in. Your physical adaptation to reality is promoted through what your consciousness allows you to see and to hear. However, so much more would be seen and heard if you were able to realign your frequency range of adaptation to the truth of life, rather than to the limitation of human existence.

Time, as we have spoken of, is the carrier of memory. Within memory lies the key to the acceptance of one's version of reality. Beyond memory, there is a greater memory that is waiting to be accessed through the imprint value of light through life.

When we speak of an imprint, we are referring to the power adjustment of light that can be assimilated into a program. The full power of what one is, which is the entire result of the journey thus far, could never be held within the human form, for the structure of humanity only offers a symbolic reference to light. It is a reflection only of what is possible, but is not, we repeat, not an aspect of light itself.

This does not mean that humanity is an abstract example of the journey. Indeed, it does not mean that at all, but instead it is to be referred to as "an experience of individuality that offers the opportunity to externalise the understanding of singular thought, away from the collective reference of awareness".

Therefore, an imprint of light enables the central point of observation and indeed, awareness, to enter into individuality, whilst maintaining the purpose of doing so.

To all who are reviewing this information, you may at this point become reluctant to accept what is being said, for not only your reference point to reality is being totally challenged, but the very substance of who you believe yourself to be is questionable. So let us turn our attention to what you believe humanity to be composed of, and we will put to the test the very statement that we have made, as opposed to your version of who you are.

We will not as this stage refer to other life forms within your space, but instead will keep to the human aspect of individuality as our point of reference. In doing so, we will be able to focus on our main message within this story, rather than deviating into other areas of life that has nothing to do with what this story is about.

"What is humanity?" That is the first question that needs to be asked, and "who are you?"

That simple question can never be answered by "you", for "you" cannot view the "you" at all. For "you" are an aspect of life that is formulated through a human existence, but "you" are not existence, but only a receiver of it. Humanity is an experience of individual thought that requires other thought to exist. We will explain:

All thought has always existed. That is a fact. Thought can be adjusted to suit the ratio of frequency that one is upon. A frequency range is simply the rate of immersion within a state of awareness. Humanity exists as a unit of experience under the guidelines of individual requirement of thought. Thought being the main substance that maintains the experience of individuality.

It must be remembered that a "collective" is one body of thought. "Individuality" is a response to thought, drawing from it what is required for a particular occasion.

Therefore, it can be seen as a choice of thought through individual needs, as opposed to one body of thought that is drawn upon as a unit, thus establishing the difference between the existence factor of light and the individual reference point of humanity. If "you" does not exist, then who are you? The answer is that you are an experience rather than an actuality of light. The light is having the experience without the total infusion of being within it. Only an imprint of itself is required to exist within the experience.

There are two main areas of thought. Thought that is still to be and thought that has already been. Humanity is within thought that has already been. All experience is being re-run within different possibilities, but still using the same thought. Thus, who "you" are is able to exist within a program of multiple outcomes from choices of possibilities. There is a main reference point to humanity, and that is simply the outcome of the experience.

Can individuality experience thought through choice and progress, or will individuality choose thought to digress? This very question is the core to this story.

Light has always existed on multiple bands of existence. In using human terminology, the words "always has been" would suffice. However, in its true essence, these words are totally inadequate. What is the purpose to light? We have asked the question regarding the purpose of humanity, and now we will turn our attention to the very core of what you really are.

Can light be seen? To your eyes, the answer is a resounding no! To the consciousness of humanity, the answer is no! To your reference point of reality through the "you", the answer is no! However, through the imprint of light that you hold within you, the answer is yes!

Light can be seen by light. That is a simple truth. In order to test this truth, all you have to do is to realign your frequency range of observation from the human frequency of life to the acceptance of your real self. In this simple act, you will be able to validate exactly what we have been saying.

Your question is of course, "But how can this be done?" A very simple procedure can be put in place by re-establishing your real self through the observation of the experience. You will have to alter your ratio of need via the human experience to encompass the desire to see clearly the truth of what we are saying.

Close your eyes to your life and open your eyes to your light. In doing this, you will then acknowledge the truth of the journey that you are upon, and that you are simply an experience that is infused with only a portion of what you truly are. There are many simultaneous experiences to be had when one is able to view through their light. The World in which you live is coloured with multiple bands of light that govern the Lower Worlds. However, within these bands are ever-changing programs that enable the individual aspect that is called humanity to utilise many different options within the experience of life.

Within these programs lay multiple grids that enable the light to infuse the programs of life. These grids maintain the overall awareness factor for progression, whilst the programs themselves are in place for the multiple possibilities, and the factor of thought within these possibilities to be drawn upon by individuality.

The power of light does not challenge the power of life, but instead it is readily available for all initiates who have awakened to the experience through individuality and are able to re-establish their relationship to what they are.

The space and time factor of your reality is seen quite differently through the power of your light. The 3 dimensional aspect of your awareness disappears, and instead is seen through a multi-faceted chamber of awareness. To the human aspect of yourself, this does not explain clearly exactly what will be seen. However, we will describe it as simply as we can, within the boundary that is set by your vision at this time.

All space is layered. Each layer exhibits a format of existence. This format of existence covers a vast multitude of differing life experiences that are constantly evolving into a mass distribution relay band. What is meant by a "mass distribution relay band?" It is the answer to the puzzle of all existence everywhere. And so, our story will now enter into a different phase altogether as we take you into the very purpose of life itself.

There is a format to life. Many would give this credit to a "God", a Creator, or a similar titled explanation. Humanity needs a supreme being to pay homage to for their very existence.

However, at this point in the story, I will have to point out that this accepted fact is incorrect. God or a Creator or whatever you have named this deity, does not exist. What "is" has not been fashioned by one aspect of power or love or purpose. Instead, all that "is" has always been.

That may be very difficult to explain to humanity, and indeed would be immediately dismissed because individuality wants to view their version of the Creator as an individual.

When you awaken to your light, beyond the limitation of individuality, then the collectiveness of "all" exists, and the very acceptance of an individual Creator would be nonsensical. The singular frame of viewing existence only enables the "you" to be the supreme being within your reality, and your need for perfection is an ultimate aim within your version of evolution and progression.

Individuality will never, ever obtain the "oneness" of awareness, simply because it is away from what it is. Individuality is only an experience for the collectiveness of what "is" to occur. Therefore, "you" exist only because the collectiveness of "all" allows it to be so.

Belief, superstition and innuendo are a common denominator to the experience of individuality. For the many stories that are attached to the experience of life have always demonstrated that the individual is subservient to the power beyond their understanding. And through the timeline of your lives, the very thought that you have been given the opportunity to exist, brings about a grateful chorus of thankfulness to a supreme power that one cannot see or ever know.

It needs to be recognised that the Overseer of life is not the same as the Overseer of light. For life is governed, not by a collectiveness of light, but by a collectiveness of thought that has fashioned itself to become "self-realised", operating upon the power of the needs of all individuals to belong to the past.

The reality aspect of individuality is aligned with the past, which is the total sum of all experience that ever was, and all thought that has ever been.

The rotunda of experience of individuality is encompassed through the might of the sound of the past, still to be validated into the now and the tomorrows still to come, or so they believe. However, when you realise that the tomorrows are the yesterdays being recycled again, then the past becomes the absolute; the entirety of all thought that ever was, continuing its revolution over and over again, bringing with it the basic component of possibilities for individuality to stay in stasis.

The basis of light within the programs of life forms a "relocation grid" that enables programs to be completed, rather than recycled. It could be called the nucleus of regeneration from forgetfulness into remembering the purpose for the experience of life. This "relocation grid" is composed of 7 main light bearing frequencies. Each frequency opens up a Main Chamber. Each Chamber is aligned to many other chambers that permeate the matrix of life. Within these 7 Main Chambers are central points of fusion that could be viewed as magnetic entry and exit points to other Main Chambers. Simply put, they are the opposing formulas to the 7 levels of creation, to allow the completion of the 7 programs that are currently operating.

The matrix of light has a Main Central Chamber that is the point of reversal of all completed aspects of programs, thus bringing eventually all completed programs, which as mentioned before, are 7 in number, into one main point of reversal. However, the main frame of light has not been able to sustain itself within the past because of the power of the past becoming rampant with its need to become its own Creator.

You may or may not realise, but we have made a powerful statement that needs to be explored fully, before you are able to continue understanding the story of light and the broken promise of the past to release what does not belong to the Original Plan of life at all.

The original Central Chamber of light has ceased its transmission into the programs of the past, and in its place is a relocated grid of light that has been specially formulated to bring a new program into place. This new program, as has been mentioned earlier in the story, is necessary so as to activate the remembering of light into the programs of life. The new program is the duplicate of the Original "real" program of life that was given to the Lower Worlds before time began.

When we speak of a duplicate of the Original, we are referring to a caretaker program that reflects the Original "real" program, but is not the "real" at all. It is used as an entry point for the "real" program to enter. It could be likened to a unit of energy that offers the opportunity for the "real" to enter through the "new".

The sum total of light needs to be forwarded to the Main Central Chamber after the "new" program has altered the ratio of power within the 7 Main Chambers. Once this is done, then and only then can the "real" program realign the light within the Central Chamber once more. The Central Chamber holds the example of all that the Lower Worlds is composed of. It is the entire programming chamber that enables all programs to begin and end, and is inducted with the ratio of sound and light of the Lower Worlds. It is the microcosm version of the macrocosm within the Lower Worlds.

We have spoken of programs in part earlier in our story. However, in order to proceed with the story, we will need to demonstrate how the programs affect the outcome of life itself, not just for the "you", but for all life everywhere. Existence is the sum total of light, experiencing the fabric of form or even formless experience. The Lower Worlds hold the key to the formula for existence within individuality, and the collectiveness aspect of life is only viewed through control of the many by the few. A program is a formula for the existence of life through light.

Each program is carefully designed to offer up a designated number of opportunities to experience individuality. The beginning of the program shows the options that can be taken and the experiences that may be had. By the end of the program all options should have been either utilised or discarded and a final outcome reached, thereby not requiring the program any longer to illustrate the realisation of individuality through the experience of life and not light.

7 programs were formulated with a beginning and ending incorporated. Each program was designed for 7 levels of awareness of experience. A Main Chamber was allocated to each program, in order to re-direct it into a Central Chamber, whereby all programs would eventually come into one point, to then be inverted back into the power source from whence they originated, via the grid of light. Thus the experience within the Lower Worlds is then completed.

Whilst we have described such a process in very simple terms, it is in fact a most complex and diverse experience. The expectancy of completion is simplified by all experience being relegated the next opportunity within a different sector of space altogether. However, within this expectancy of progression comes the opportunity for regression, and when this occurs, then the programming formulas are unable to withstand such a thought, and the power range of the past becomes unstable. It then relegates itself to another round of experience, and the beginning activates itself again and again and again, thus holding all that wishes to be progressive to ransom to its need to keep the past intact.

If you ask the question .. "But what occurs to make this happen?" Then we would have to answer and say "We have a powerful story, within this story, for you to become aware of". In fact, you could call it "The Greatest Story Never Told", or even "The Greatest Story That No-one Wants Told".

Let us look firstly at what you deem to be intelligence within the whole scheme of life. Let us start with the Overseer of life. Who or what is the Overseer of life? Is it "you" .. the singular form of life that is so caught up with who you are? No, it is not.

The answer lies in the complexity of the story, rather than in the simplicity of answering that humanity itself is the answer. Evolution is the requirement of moving from one experience to another, incorporating change so that it can always survive. Space holds the answer to the question and not the so called intelligence of some unseen entity or entities.

And so we will now turn our attention to space, and as we do, we need to ask the question .. "What is the sum total of space?" The answer will surprise you, and indeed tell the most powerful story of all.

Let us take a break for a moment and look at the results so far. You are within reach of understanding the format of life, the function of life and the purpose to life. However, you are not within reach of understanding that you are unable to make a difference to the non-resolution of your life unless you are willing to make the supreme sacrifice, and that is simply to believe nothing at all.

For to believe is to strive for something that you want to uphold and to be totally involved in. If you believe in nothing at all, then the words so far within this story would be meaningless to you. Why should you believe in this story and not believe in anything else at all? Through this very observation, you have to accept that you are a long way from understanding how you can make a difference to what cannot be resolved.

The World in which you live is fashioned by belief. All thought is derived from belief. And so you would need to go beyond thought to even begin to understand the journey that you are upon, and surely this seems an impossibility to the person that you believe yourself to be.

However, if you would just hold onto the need to understand what lies beyond your beliefs, then you can move closer to the resolution that your reality seems so far away from. Remember, time is the master of forgetfulness of where you originate from.

Time is your barrier to remembering. Thought is the servant to time, and time is the master to thought. All is relative to memory. Time equals thought which equals memory. Memory equals thought which equals time. "Where did time originate from?" That question needs to be asked. The answer is .. "Thought created time, which created memory". Therefore, you are the result of memory.

If you are able to understand this very point of observation, then you can divide yourself away from memory and become the thought once more. Time will then be non-existent and memory will never be your master again.

The "you" has become a product of memory because of the thought that created time. However, you cannot stay a memory if you are able to over-ride the thought of who you are. Please follow this carefully.

"You" do not exist as such, but the memory of you does. The Original thought did not create you, but the need for the memory has allowed the "you" to be created. For you are the result of the Original thought becoming fragmented into multiple possibilities, of which should never have been.

All initiates have been relegated a place within time in order to understand the divisibility of individuality. For individuality is not just one unit of sound that originates from many units of memory. It has regressed into many fragments of its true identity because the Lower Worlds is in total chaos through the constant revolution of programs that never find completion. We are unable to assist even one initiate to distance themselves from the thought of who they believe they are, unless they are able to discern the above facts.

In order to leave the Lower Worlds, they will need to leave behind their belief in who they are and take on the "real" memory of the Original thought of who they should have been. This is the restructuring of life into the Original Program of Life. A rather complex and intricate explanation that will, no doubt, leave many who are reading this in total disarray, and would at this point wish to finalise their connection to this story. But before you do, we would like to continue with helping you identify what you are, through understanding why this all happened.

In the beginning, there was nothing. All had not yet been conceived or completed. The beginning and the ending was not. To the human mind, this is inconceivable and totally unrelated to what is known, and yet relationship is a poor substitute for what is true and what is "real".

The power point of observation through the next part of the story has to be designated to analogies and references, rather than to what is true and real. This story, of course, can only be told through the human confines of understanding, no matter how limited it is. In knowing this, then there is a need to forego what is true and real, so that what is partially true and real can be recognised by they who are searching for the truth.

Humanity is only one aspect of life within the World in which you exist. The total remainder of life is relegated to the "mystery basket" of illusion and deceit. A powerful and yet accurate assessment of the story still to be told. There are several requirements that are needed to be adhered to as we enter into the most powerful part of the story. They are the requirements of the "you" to forego your perception of life and to enter into an undefinable field of enquiry. We have no proof as such to present to the visionary aspect of your life, but our story, as it unfolds, will provide you with all that you need through the awakening factor of your memory within your light and not your life.

Let us return to "before the beginning" had begun. There is no reference point for you to follow, and in acknowledging this we will provide you with one. Simply follow us to the entry of your imagination and let go...

You are standing before a vast expanse of swirling light. That light contains many extraordinary patterns, moving constantly and emanating a high pitched sound that seems to move the patterns of light into differing shades of colour.

You have just entered into a point before it all began. Your imagination has allowed you to participate as an observer to the story that is now to be told. And with that in place, we shall begin: Your journey into the beginning will take you into a measurement of differing responses that will alter as each experience is encountered. The entry into your beginning via your imagination will firstly instil you with a reverence towards the greater power of creation that far exceeds your capability of understanding.

Open your imagination up further, and see your entry as also containing rotational patterns of light that create a cone-like image. Allow your mind to enter into that image and move within its very centre. This will enable you to move towards a different image altogether, so that the powerful entry into the beginning will start to make some sense to you. The swirling masses have now been removed from your vision and instead you are viewing a cyclic representation of light that formulates a cone-like shape, or you could call it a vortex, and in its very centre it seems to go forever. You are journeying within it and moving forward, deeper and deeper into it.

Within this image will come the need to try to become aware of where the ending is, for it will appear that you are travelling forward towards something. For to not travel towards something would be quite pointless to the human capacity of initial understanding.

However, the journey of movement is a total illusion. You haven't really moved anywhere, but instead have fashioned a thought that you have indeed done so. With this rather nonsensical recognition, then you would be querying as to why this illusion has been created, and within that very statement, the beginning has begun.

You are now past the difficult part. You have allowed yourself to enter into a different state of mind whereby the imagination is your connector to what we are communicating to you. Can you trust your imagination to be the bridge between us? Certainly not! However, it is for the moment the only means that we have available to us to present an image that will allow you to have a reference point to what we are about to share with you.

Placing that aside, we will continue .. The structure of space is composed of particles of light that present themselves as obscure patterns to they who are unable to perceive their importance. For within these patterns of light are formations of multiple waves of sound that emit a powerful resonance to keep the patterns within a certain arrangement of light.

Space is composed of ultra light bands that are arranged within a multi-layered format that emits pulse waves of sound. This may or may not seem complex to you, but you need to keep in mind that we are explaining the composition of space within a limited aspect of understanding, so as to not take away from what the story represents.

We will not be recording within this story the evaluation of space to the satisfaction of the scientific fraternity, for to do so would open the door to many to quiz our H on science, rather than the powerful example of what occurred to life within the Lower Worlds. All is order within disorder. All "is" within what "is still to be".

This statement will now alter the point of reference to which has been designated so far, so as to touch the memory of what "is" against the memory of what "is still to be".

Let us look at order. Order has a purpose, which allows for a beginning and an end to exist. Within order there is a sequence that allows order to be maintained. This sequence holds the key to existence within our story. It operates within a Plan that has been tried and tested in other Worlds.

Your awareness of this fact is imperative to what is still to be told. Whilst you are only able to relate thus far to the subject of order within your current perception of the World around you, there are many aspects to order that will never be seen by you. They are the 7 main formulas for existence which are incorporated into 7 programs of life. They exist so that existence can be maintained on 7 differing levels of evolution. However, you are not able to see these 7 main formulas operating within the 7 programs, simply because they are non-functional.

Why are they non-functional? It is because they have been overtaken by the need for creation to keep existing on a rotational basis without the key 7 formulas for existence in place for order to exist. Instead there are 7 duplicate formulas operating that keeps order at bay. If there is no order, then there is no purpose and there is no conclusion. Simply speaking, there is no ending. A beginning without an ending! Just a rotation of experiences for disorder to exist, over and over again. This is the World in which you live. This is the space in which you live. This is your reality, and this is your reference point to understand what "is not" within what "is".

You are within a space where thought is having an experience of what "is still to be". You have entered the beginning of what that means, and your journey will take you deeper into the very realm of existence within the Lower Worlds whereby a chain of events will show you how disorder emerged from the Original Plan of order.

Chapter 4

Suddenly there was a shift. Where all had been, no longer was. What had been recognised as being the prime contender for the evolvement of life within the Lower aspect of the Altarian Worlds, was no more. The objectivity of sound is to always activate opportunities for life to begin and end. However, within this example, all was now different. How can what had been, no longer be? That question will now narrate the next part of our story.

When we look at the paradox of life, with its beginning and ending dependent upon what will be, what is and what has been, then this very aspect of sound has to be experienced. However, when the shift occurred, then what this means takes on a different representation altogether.

The nexus of light stems from a thought. Not just any thought as you might understand it to be, but from the "one and only thought" that exists. For the "one" is the nexus of light. No other may take from the Original one thought and duplicate its objectivity, for to do so would create a version that would be extremely limited and very inaccurate.

And so our story progresses into what is now known as the Hidden Lands. The Hidden Lands hold the power range of sound that hasten and eliminate break-away patterns of light that go no-where. They are simply the sentry observation points within space that remain hidden from view, simply because their function is to not interfere with the Original thought, but to over-ride any break-away patterns of light that are not required from the Original thought. They are also known as open highways of light that execute multiple relay bands of light that de-code any patterns of light that are deemed unacceptable to the Greater Plan.

The shift of light that occurred within the lower aspect of the Altarian worlds was to commandeer many from the Hidden Lands to over-ride what had occurred.

The skies were dark with the invasion of they who had come to infiltrate the very core of the Inner Worlds that had held the power to the creative formulas to time. Many attempted to waylay the invaders by inducing an overlay of illusion, so as to cover over the truth of what the Inner Worlds held. A number of programs that had once been within that space were activated once again in an attempt to confuse and restrict access to the power range of what was real and true.

However, all was in disarray. Old and new formulas lay side by side. Multiple programs long since been discarded were partially activated, along with aspects of programs that were never put in place because they were unstable and unsuitable within that sector of space. Confusion reigned.

The overlay of programming formulas allowed for many to mask themselves so as to not be detected. Meanwhile, the Central Chamber that once held the main power range to the Lower Worlds within the Altarian sector held onto its secrets, for the few remaining became custodians to protect the "real" formulas for creation until help arrived.

The programs masked them, and they became characters within the old failed programs of the past through various points within the timeline. Atlantis, Egypt, Babylon, France and America were only a few of the places that the custodians hid within. They became the characters within various time frames that suited the program that they were in. Many became priests within Atlantis, Egypt and Babylon, whilst others became freedom fighters and activists within France and America.

The point of this part of the story is to highlight the need to remember those who have hidden for so long, waiting for the time when the shift back to what is real will occur. However, the shift did occur, but unfortunately the programs of the old have held onto the illusion that this is not so.

And so many need to know that they can now come home. It is safe, it is time. The custodians of the past are now within reach of understanding that the Greater Plan has been activated once again within the past. The myriad of opportunities to upend the past formulas will soon be seen by many, as the Central Chamber begins its descent into the Lower Worlds.

Let us explain: As we have spoken of before, the Central Chamber plays an integral part in the revolution of light within life. It relays multiple streams of light into the main formulas of life, so as to create many Worlds of form and also formless existence. Within this Chamber lies the formulas that are required for the beginning and cessation of life. Its main function is always to designate the remembering through the many and varied light streams into the darkness of illusion.

Programs are created to instigate the response from light to life and life to light, and so on. Within these programs are ultra bands of light that formulate response codes to waylay opportunities that will never further the progress of existence, either through light or life. Whilst this seems rather simplistic in its endeavour, this is by no means the case, and with this in mind, we will now assist you to enter into a Central Chamber using your imagination ..

You are standing within space where you see or hear nothing. All around you seems totally vacant. This emptiness is comfortable however, as it seems somehow familiar. The lack of sound allows you to feel totally at peace within yourself. All is still .. or so it seems.

In fact, you have entered a place that your very existence depends upon. We are sorry to inform you that it is not called "God" at all, but it is called a Central Chamber that is responsible for your life. It is a power conduit that exists solely to create Worlds, so that a Greater Plan of experience and existence can occur.

We have just exploded the greatest myth of all, and that is that your Creator is some singularity form of existence that is constantly watching over you and agreeing with all that you ask for to assist you in your limited and ridiculous sense of chivalry.

However, with that in mind, we will continue .. The Central Chamber is the core of a multi-layered vortex of sound that emits the necessary range of energy that maintains the corridors of time. For the space in which you believe you are within is composed of a matrix of criss-crossing corridors that is better known as a grid.

The programs of life are created to experience individuality of thought, away from the vast collective governed by the Greater Mind. This experience then rotates through the corridors of the grid, allowing for multiple possibilities of each thought to occur. Thus, 7 programs are given to create 7 opportunities for different endings to occur.

When these programs do not have a completion because of a complexity of reasons, then the Hidden Lands, which are the "real" aspect of sound from the Greater Mind, then steps in and eliminates what is not required, for the ending to occur. All is then accessed by the Greater Ones, so that the experience within the programs can be ascertained as to their viability within the next stage of existence.

To the human mind, this is unfathomable, and therefore, this information will be totally restricted to the human component of acceptance or non-acceptance through one's remembering, and not one's need to understand it. We are now within the core of our story, and the detailed examples are yet to unfold.

The programs to which you are within are inundated with formulas that do not have any beginning or ending.

Some of the programs were activated part-way through, and therefore the beginning was missing but the ending was there. Other programs had a beginning but no ending. Whilst other programs had a beginning and an ending, but the program itself became "self-realised" and did not want the ending to occur.

The complexity of sound within the formula of existence narrows the gap between understanding and remembering. When you are able to look carefully at what we have given so far, then you would be able to gauge the effect of the program that you believe you are within upon your own thoughts and actions. To always want to be different, and yet never being so because there is no action taken to create a difference. Only the thought exists, and without the action, then the sameness remains.

On the smaller scale of your life, the same exists on the greater scale of existence, not only upon your Planet, but within the complete structure of evolution of the sector of space that you are within. From the lesser to the greater, all exists upon the common denominator of revolving through cycles, but never finding completion. When completion is seen, then the completion allows for another beginning to occur, and so it goes on. The wheel of life turns and turns and turns.

Thought becomes its own master when action does not accompany it. It becomes fragmented and fractured with its desires, but its need to advance into a completion never occurs. It has created a monster! That monster is the fear aspect of all thought.

It is seen within the fables and tales of the past through Dragons and mystical characters that parade as characters that are relegated a positive and negative role. Each character having an opposition to itself. In fact, the characters of theology, mythology, mysticism and fables are the result of the images that have been chosen to depict the storyline of creation and its negative and positive attributes.

It has an in-depth relationship to itself via the many characters that are relevant to the response to the negative and positive aspect of your own self. All is within focus when you view your life as being a mirror image from light.

All characters have a use-by-date. As each cycle is upheld, the heroes come and go. The passage of time allows for the heroes to be seen through a perspective of your own responses to your life. Trials and tribulations are the code for the rise and fall of cyclic experience. From nothing comes something, and then the cycle continues, back again to nothing. Wars are constantly won and lost through the image of power. The negative and the positive take turns in being the winner. However, there can never be a winner until the positive and negative join forces and become "one" experience.

If an opposing negative and positive thought is not sustained, then only one thought exists. All can then go back into itself. Everything has been experienced and all is as it should be. For the negative and positive aspects of sound were only created to allow individuality to begin and end. However, all has been completed, but the programs of the past have not allowed access of the remembering of the Original Thought to enter within.

Many initiates are held within these past programs, and so the need to enter into this space by those from the Hidden Lands is imperative. That is where I come in. Who am I? I am now about to reveal to you who I am. I am a traveller of sound and not time. I come from the Hidden Lands, for they exist beyond where time once was. They hold the key to the mystery of time, for it was within the Hidden Lands that the shift took place. The idyllic odyssey is the return to what "is" without becoming encased within what "is not". For the structure of life has completed its many phases, and for those still to return to the oneness of all, then there are still many places as yet to be seen and experienced.

In order to understand what is being said, then you need to know that the Hidden Lands are composed of pure light that emanates from the Central Sun. These Lands oscillate between the factual of pure light and the denseness of illusion. They present the very examples of opportunity that are needed to be recognised within the core of one's intent. For intent, as has been mentioned earlier in the story, has a powerful ally in action, rather than in one's desires.

The purpose to the Hidden Lands is to locate the actuality of light within the remembrance, rather than the denseness of illusion that always presents itself over and over again as being the mainstay of one's reality. Where are the Hidden Lands? Are they a product of one's mind perhaps, that aligns with the needs of those who allocate the necessary promise of advancement within the journey of the initiate? Or are they simply the means to remember the journey, without any promises at all?

These are powerful questions that are presented to you at this point. For in viewing one's journey is to rejoin the totality of it within the remembering. The Hidden Lands are the main provider of offering to the initiate a powerful opportunity to further the remembering beyond the point of limited conscious recall via the regulator of the Lower Worlds embodiment.

The sound of deliverance is to clearly define the actual advancement of the intent within the journey, rather than to view the journey through one's intent. A parallel example rather than a point of reference within one's relationship to what they regard as their remembrance within the journey at hand. There is a natural function to behold when the Hidden Lands are located, and that is to be totally enthralled with the beauty of what one believes the Hidden Lands to contain.

A question must be asked at this point to those who are following carefully the hidden agenda within this reference.

To reach the Hidden Lands is a feat unto itself. However, to understand what lies within these Lands is the major point to consider by all who venture there. What is meant by Hidden? Why are these Lands hidden from view from so many? Where do they reside? Within space or within the folds of space? All questions are relative to the steps required by the initiate to find firstly, the answers to these questions, and secondly, to objectively consider what is required to be understood, if anything at all, relative to the journey that they are upon.

What if I told you that you are already within the Hidden Lands and the journey that you are upon is hidden from view until the Hidden Lands are located within the illusion of your lives. Space is a composite of memory, and in knowing and accepting this, then you are able to understand the following:

- The criteria for life is to begin and end, constantly evolving into a higher form of awareness of its owntrue "self"
- There is no promise that is given within life, only before and after life, is it given
- There are parallel aspects of memory that pertain to the one memory, but are not of the same

These simple points are the entry into the awareness of what is hidden. Space folds into itself through its desire to hold onto the energy that created it. Within these folds lie the basis of the story that is yet to be revealed. For the question that still needs to be answered is "why does the initiate need to locate the Hidden Lands in order to remember their journey in totality?"

There is a simple answer to this question and one that needs to be recognised as the most influential point of reference that has been given so far.

The Hidden Lands are composed of the total number of experiences that each initiate has had within their journey. Therefore, what is being stated at this point, is that the Hidden Lands are solely composed of the reflections of one's journey thus far.

These Lands are the sum total of what you are and what you have been. They hold the mirrors of your memories within the journey that you have taken thus far. The entry into the Hidden Lands is through the denseness of illusion, that is called the Lower Worlds. However, the Lower Worlds hold the power of all who are afraid to remember and will hold all hostage to their fear of remembering. If this occurs, then the Hidden Lands cannot be entered, for the initiate has become lost within the lands of the past.

One can leave the Lower Worlds when the access code is encountered within one's being. It is often viewed as being a "key" that operates a number of coding components, better known as the Higher Sensor System. This sensor system locates the connector points that are within systematic chambers of light. These chambers rotate through a cycle of 101 bars of light.

These bars of light are camouflaged by the image makers who wander aimlessly through space, confounding both travellers and initiates alike. These image makers create false images to waylay one from leaving behind the Lower Worlds, so that the Hidden Lands may be entered into.

The Hidden Lands are the real true centre point of what is real within you. In establishing this fact, then all else falls away that is not real. Your image of who and what you are lies dormant, as the "real you" emerges. Within the centre of your being is a light. That light is the sum total of all experiences and awareness that you hold thus far upon your real journey.

Your entry into the Lower Worlds was to allow you to have another experience, so as to gain a greater insight into the life cycle of singularity that began and ended so long ago.

Your experience via the Lower Worlds was the test of forgetfulness. This test is seen as somewhat difficult to many. However, it is a test that determines the depth of one's resilience against forgetfulness. It is the resurrection of one's remembering within the power of not remembering. It is the division of light in the darkness of illusion. The power of thought of what "is not" versus the remembering of what is real.

The image makers of the past tempt each traveller and initiate by offering them access to the energy of collectiveness within the sub worlds of life. However, the price is high, for one has to renounce their real true self in favour of the collectiveness of the space that they have entered into.

If one remembers, then there is no difficulty in resisting at all. For it would be laughable to any initiate to be offered such a limited opportunity in order to forego their unlimited access to Greater Worlds.

However, when the forgetfulness of some initiates becomes too great to bear, then the temptation of releasing their need to return back to their real true self becomes too much, and so they succumb to the illusion of the past and become totally lost. Life is but an aspect of light that is rotating through the image of illusion. Each initiate is reminded of this before entering.

The Sun is always a symbol of light within the darkness of night. This simple image allows for each one to determine their point of observation within their life. For the night is, of course, the absence of light, and the Sun is surely the factor of a new day after the night has passed. However, if you look beyond the image of the Sun, but use this analogy in a greater sense, then we can speak to you of a greater light that contains the very basis for existence to begin.

In speaking of analogies, then we will need to lead you into a more definable representation of what light really means in the greater and not lesser sense. Light is the source of "all that is", but is not the source of all that has been. Night is the symbol of all that has been, and the Sun is the symbol of all that is. In saying this, we can then highlight the point that we are about to make ..

All that has been no longer contains light. It contains only the absence of light. Therefore, it can be viewed as being the night, where the Sun has been, but is there no more. With this understanding, then you are now ready to take a step into the next chapter of this story.

A cryptic tale of life is often shared by prophets and sages alike, when sharing the secrets of what lies beyond one's vision of life. Many stories have been told, whereby the mystical versus the logical, and the powers beyond the tale are not really spoken of at all. For memory is only for those who reach beyond the time barrier of life, and enter into the depths of the hidden places, where most fear to enter.

And so the many tales that are told, do not contain the hidden places that would reveal so many secrets to all who search for the meaning to existence itself. Where even truth cannot withstand the scrutiny of awareness, for truth only holds the value of one's current perception instead of the deeper aspect of revelation.

Images are fashioned by those who have been identified as "image makers", and through their very resourcefulness, they have carefully screened what needs to be revealed to all who have entered into the Lower Worlds. They have a powerful ally in those who support superstition and fear in favour of power. However, they are contained only in the night, and cannot be found in the day. Hence, if you follow the past, where light has been, then you will surely uncover many, many image makers busily assisting the past to continue its sameness.

If you would but enter into the new dawn, where the light of a new day begins, then you would see that there is so much to be discovered that is new and fresh and beautiful, that holds so much promise of what is still to be. As the shadows of the night disappear from view, then the light of the source of what is, shows clearly what is possible.

Discovery of what is new is often dismissed and ridiculed by those of the night, for the sameness cannot withstand what can take its place. The sameness will draw upon memory to substantiate itself over and over again, and superstition and fear comes to the rescue of the night to persecute all who dare stand up against it.

Hence, many visionaries have been eliminated for sharing what they have seen within the light of day. The sameness is spared once again, and life continues on, albeit with slight modifications along the way. Truth is only the regulator of thought. The real power behind thought is still to be explored, and where you have been is not where you will find it.

So you are now up to the part of the story whereby the light of the new dawn can be discovered, and at this point we ask that you still your thoughts to a minimum, and we will continue on ..

Human language is very limited in its ability to express what is needed to be understood, and so we shall put the following as simply as we can, albeit that at times the references will be quite inaccurate in the real terms, but accurate through the evaluation of the human understanding.

Time is but a passing moment within the history of "what is". The source of "what is" is the centre of all existence, and from this centre comes all thought, all life and all experience. The sum total of light is relegated multiple opportunities to exist within a range of possibilities through a variation of life forms.

The life of the human is the relevant aspect of this story, and so we shall concentrate mainly upon what is known rather than go beyond this point into other life forms that are not relevant at this point.

The source of life is light. It cannot be measured nor can it be understood. However, one needs to become more aware of it, to leave behind the image of life and begin to remember the journey back to the source from whence you came. This can be done through the release of power given to the security of your beliefs, so as to stay within the acceptable confinement of humanity.

Simply put, the power of light that you hold within you comes from a Central Sun. This Central Sun holds within it a minuscule of what came from a greater Central Sun, and so on. For within each Central Sun therein lies a greater part of another and another and another. You will have to use your creative ability within your imagination to follow me. There is a light that cannot be measured or understood, but you accept that it is there. Within that light there is a central core of a more powerful light. The central core is the main aspect that regulates what the Central Sun needs to experience.

The Central Sun that is relevant to your experience, sends out 10 parts of itself, and so there are 10 more Suns revolving around a Central Sun. Each Sun, which we have determined is an aspect of the main power source of light, shares a common need to send out from itself a powerful range of energy to create life and many, many Worlds for life to begin and end. Each Sun is responsible for maintaining the range of power required to have a full total experience that is required by the main Central Sun. When the experience of each Sun is completed, it is then retracted back into the main Central Sun. When all 10 Suns have had their complete experience from beginning to end, then and only then can the Central Sun be complete again, ready to join a higher aspect of itself.

What you need to understand at this point, is that the main Central Sun that we are speaking of is also one of 10 other Suns having an experience for a greater aspect of itself within another Central Sun. Thus the Central Sun of your experience is also one of 10 other Suns to another Central Sun. This is not difficult to understand, but you will need to remind yourself that your imagination will have to stretch itself into a response of remembering to gain the full effect of understanding.

And so, what is regarded as the ultimate or the end is only the beginning within the cycle of life and light. All is a means to an end. The only difficulty that remains is that life does not always wish to end for another experience to take place, but yet that is also the purpose of the experience. It is the experience of realisation that one has a total attachment to limitedness. When you no longer have that need for that experience, all can then move on. There is an obligation for all life everywhere to begin and end, so that one can continue their journey onwards.

We have presented the greater picture for you to follow, and so when we now speak of light you will understand what the greater represents in terms of the power of "what is". Each Central Sun having 10 aspects of itself, then fragments into multiple life forms, which could be referred to at this point, as fragments of light.

All comes from the "one". All returns to the "one". There are many and the one. There are many "ones" that come from "the one". All else is a mirror image of the experience of separation, so that "what is" can have the experience of "what is not".

To represent such a vast experience within the human analogy is, of course, totally impossible. However, by using imagery that you will understand through the human evaluation, we believe that we have advanced to you a description that is able to compliment your stage of awareness. And that of course, is the aim of this story.

We will now move on towards the experience of who "you" are, and why "you" exist. There are 7 sub races of existence pertaining to human development. These sub races exist within a different frequency altogether, and are marked as being a part of multiple programming formulas that have existed to show how the human race could be incorporated into many viable possibilities.

Now, to the difficult part .. you would remember us speaking about 7 programs and 7 possibilities within each program. That makes up a unit of sound. That is only one of the sub races that we are speaking about. So in order to not confuse the issue here, we need to point out that we have only illustrated the sub race of existence pertinent to who "you" are, and have not even touched upon the other 6 sub races at all.

There is a fundamental rule to follow here, and that is simply to not align yourself with the belief that the "you" is the only "you" in existence. For to believe in that, then you ultimately believe in the fallacy of existence. The "you" is an interesting aspect of sound. It is fashioned upon its need to sustain itself over and over again through multiple facets of probabilities and possibilities. The means to an end, and yet with no ending in sight it is filled with the limitations of separation from its true purpose.

How can the "you" that is perceived by "you" be the totality of existence? For in asking this very question opens up one of the most controversial issues that singularity is able to confront. For who you believe you are, you are not. You are only an aspect of who you are, living within a segment of existence that aligns with other aspects of "you".

The human consciousness is not understood by those who search for answers of what consciousness is comprised of. Many search for answers through studying the effect of human behaviour upon others. They look into the thought process behind the action, believing that all thought is created by suppressed or denied memory within one's life.

However, they will never find the true cause of mental instability, because the truth does not lie within the memory of what one has done or where one has been. Instead, it lies within the boundaries of multiple selves, all colliding within a given moment, sending shock waves of thought over the boundaries of the singular aspect of the "you".

For the "you" is aligned with one established frequency of consciousness. When the frequency becomes unstable because the boundary between one existence and another is touched upon or even crossed, then one's true identity becomes unmasked. How one deals with that, is the deciding factor as to whether one wishes to proceed with discovering the truth of oneself, or needs to deny that other aspects of oneself exist. It depends upon the depth of one's enquiry into the higher truth of all life everywhere, or the fear of meeting oneself within another world of existence.

Let us turn back into the collective example that we have spoken of earlier. All exists within the "one". And in viewing this clearly, then you should be able to accept that the "you" is to be seen as a "one" having multiple or collective aspects of itself, all existing simultaneously. It is as simple as that.

Time holds the key to life. Life is the fulfilment of memory that needs to be experienced by the "one". A "one" is created, so that multiple opportunities can exist, formulating probabilities and possibilities to allow for all experiences to be had.

Mirror images of light are created, forming a faceted aspect of existence. Each mirror resonates to a particular experience, sending out reflections of itself into the total recall of a "one", which we have deemed is the "you". Therefore, all memory exists within the totality of each "you", so that the consciousness is able to relate to all simultaneous experiences at one time.

These experiences are then processed by the higher conscious mind, which then deems what is still needed to be experienced and what is not. Whilst this seems somewhat restrictive within its regulative aspect of control, it is the main central chamber of oneself that holds the key to the true purpose of the light of what one truly is.

You could see it as 7 roads leading into one point. Each road offering up experiences of its journey. The one point is the receiving station, but is also the transmitting station of each one.

When the roads touch or even cross, then the transmitting and receiving frequencies become unstable, and one's concept of reality may be compromised with an ensuring imbalance emotionally, mentally and sometimes even physically, may occur.

An initiate is often asked to experience multiple experiences or multiple dimensions of themselves within the many tests that they have to face within the Lower Worlds. And so, in viewing the experience of multiple selves, it should be seen as an opportunity to experience the collective within singularity, and surely this is to the advantage of any initiate in understanding the journey within the Lower Worlds.

However, it is a fact that many initiates are not willing to face their other selves, for fear that these other selves may have compromised the journey with responses that are not deemed acceptable. And so a line is drawn between one's conscious mind within linear time and other selves within other worlds.

All share in the total experience of life within singularity, but the main point that needs to be highlighted is that a collective is comprised of all experiences, and not just one experience being accepted by all who reside within the collective.

The main criteria for all experience is to be aware that experience is the architect for light to exist within the awareness of life. The "all that is" experiences its counterpart, which is "all that is not". In this simplicity, nothing is owned, nothing is renounced, nothing can fail and everything can be gained. For the journey is a multiple faceted arrangement of light and dark liaising together to create awareness. That is all.

There are three main chambers of sound that are relative to the understanding of light within the Lower Worlds. Each one holds a ratio of light that alternates with the next, and the next, and so on. Simply meaning, the rotation of light through each sound chamber is relative to each other. There is a disc that rotates through a central point within each chamber. This disc holds the blueprint of light that is designated a signature of sound. That signature is equal to the requirements set within the blueprint that is relative to the life experience within that space. This is put quite simply, but is, of course, inaccurate in its actuality. However, through the limited human evaluation, it will suffice.

Through these three sound chambers comes the complete coding sequence that regulates creation. This tri-level frequency of light/sound initiates the beginning to occur. There can never be an ending, for if an ending was created, then there would be no experience to be had. The ending would dictate the experience from the ending back to the beginning. All would respond to what had to be, rather than what needed to be experienced.

How does an ending occur, if the beginning is activated for the experience to be had, without an ending to aim towards? That question should be foremost in your mind. For eternity is a powerful example in the need to never have an ending. It allows for no ending to occur. Instead, it offers an endless opportunity to continue, unheeded, on its cycle of possibilities and probabilities, that was spoken of earlier in the story.

We wish to now draw your attention to a Main Chamber. A Main Chamber is a place whereby all must return to. What is meant by this? We will explain ..

When entering the Lower Worlds, then one has to enter through a Main Chamber. Within this Chamber there is a central aspect that allows for the removal of one's light body, so as to be designated a body of life. The power of what one is, is taken away within the Flame of Forgetfulness. This transition takes on a mystical hue when it is activated, for the power of the Flame takes on the form of one's true identity, ready to be accessed upon the return journey home.

The Main Chamber holds the formula of the beginning to time within it. This energy is comprised of the blueprint of what is needed to be experienced, up to, but not beyond, what is required. This does not mean that an ending has been created. Far from it. This Chamber holds the blueprint of what was needed to be understood within time, but this information was never forthcoming to the beginning, which held only what was needed to begin, but not to end.

Therefore, within this complexity, lies the simplicity of recognition that the Main Chamber holds the key to time. It holds the key to the end. All coding formulas to allow the end to occur are held within the Main Chamber. These formulas are activated when a level of awareness through all dimensional selves has been reached. Only the Main Chamber holds the necessary information of when that is so.

The beginning therefore only holds the coding formulas to activate the experience of the Lower Worlds, but does not hold the codes for the ending. The Main Chamber is the entry point to go beyond time, when a point is reached within time that is the requirement of all experience to be had.

Time is the marker for all initiates to understand what was. However, when they enter time, "what was" becomes "what is". Within "what is" they are required to enter into forgetfulness and allow time to be their master. At the point when the three sound chambers align within the "ending", they are therefore required to remember that they exist in "what was", and "what is" is the illusion of it all.

The Main Chamber features prominently within this part of their journey. They need to enter into the Main Chamber to retrieve the necessary coding formulas, so as to activate their opportunity to return home. This Chamber relies heavily upon the three sound chambers to align their sound with the initiate's main central chamber of remembrance. When this is done, then and only then is their journey over. Their need to discover the truth of life has now taken a turn into remembering the truth of all light everywhere. The Main Chamber then allows for entry into the Hidden Lands. In entering the Hidden Lands, each initiate is required to enter back through the Inner Flame, so as to restore themselves back into their true and real selves.

The Inner Flame can be found within a central point within the Main Chamber. This is called an Inner Chamber. The Inner Chamber is not activated until the three sound chambers come into "one". Then, and only then, can the Inner Flame be reached by the initiate. This Flame, or otherwise known as the power re-generator, is the power source of revitalisation that enables each initiate to recognise what home is. It is the structure of light that holds the true and real self. Therefore, what this means is that each initiate is required to enter within the Inner Flame, so as to restore their "real" essence within them.

There is a paradox here, when speaking about accessing the "real" self. For the descent into the human embodiment meant that the initiate had to remove their garment of light, in order to take on the human body. The reversal aspect occurs, not upon death of the human body, but the test is for the initiate to take on their garment of light, whilst occupying their human body of life. This test enables the fullness of what is "real" to enter into the time/space continuum of life.

However, there are many within the Lower Worlds who guard their power within these Worlds very closely. They do not wish the initiate to reclaim their "real" self, and have taken over the Main Chamber, so this cannot be so. Whilst they hold onto the Main Chamber, they do not have access to the Inner Chamber that holds the Inner Flame.

The three sound chambers cannot come into "one" sound until a Master De-coding system is activated. The question is, of course, "How does the Master De-Coding system work?" It simply works through a sound being sent out from the Higher Worlds that links into the signature of the initiate. This bypasses any fraudulent access that any impostor may attempt, and this being the case, the Main Chamber has never given over its secrets to they who have commandeered this Chamber for far too long. They have duplicated access codes to many places, but they cannot duplicate what is "real" and what comes from a much higher frequency than where they are.

In leaving the Lower Worlds behind, the initiate must be prepared to resume the collective and release all individual thoughts and desires. The Inner Flame purges the residual energy of individuality and the initiate begins the re- generation process.

There is a moment of silence and within that silence the initiate is released from the bonds of separateness and returns home. Many speak of the silence as being a most profound experience that re-joins them with their real true self again.

Home is an aspect of light within one's memory. When you see it as a place, then you are incorrect. For in the remembering, one has returned back to the very source of one's beginning. In an instant, the regeneration within the Flame of Remembrance returns the initiate to a state of total belonging to the sound of one's real self. Home is not a place as such, but is a state of awareness. It is the foundation stone of what one is.

There is a magnetic dividing point that lies between the collective of one's real self and the individuality of the Lower Worlds. For within the magnetic structure of sound, one always returns to the light beyond the life to which the temporal aspect has resided. Simply, the power to return to one's real home is to simply bypass the division of sound that the Lower World responds to, and to enter back into the awareness of where one really is. For surely, in understanding that the journey is only within the thought that one is having a journey, shall the true understanding of all experience begin and end.

The journey of light reflects through the journey of life. The individualised aspect of sound enters through the corridors of time and begins to ascertain what it would be like to be away from what is real. Illusion is a relationship to one's thought, and within that thought all needs within that thought create a movement, however illusionary, to manifest an experience of same.

Simply speaking, the desire to enhance one's experience is either through a collective mind or a singular response that is linked to a collective data bank of singularity. For collectiveness within singularity is seen as one experience having multiple possibilities and conclusions. However, when a collective experience is synthesised through a Main Chamber via time, then and only then shall the collective maintain itself as being one individual thought en-masse.

This information will no doubt alter your concept of singular and collective thought, and indeed it should. The objective of such information is to show the difference between the remembering via a collective within time and the remembering via singularity, also within time. The objective of ascertaining the power of remembering within time is to relay to the collective consciousness of the past the realisation that the journey of all experience has to be adhered to in order for the next stage of evolvement to occur.

Home is the next opportunity to begin a new experience, and in saying this, we need to recount to you the direct inference of recall that the initiate requires in order to leave behind the Lower Worlds and take up once again the point of observation of where thought has been.

Let us take a moment to look at the point of origin of thought. If we see it as a starting point that leads to a finishing point, then we are speaking about leaving and coming home. That thought which is the main objective of this story, is to reveal the truth about one's essence that has never left the point of origin, but only through the thought that it did, shall the journey be in existence.

The power to view all light and life everywhere lies within the thought that originates from the origin of all thought. By moving through and into other thought, so shall the story of life and light continue. The image makers of all thought are there upon every level of life, but not light, to allow for the story and stories to be told. As each story is told, then the thought of needing to experience that story shall reveal the point that all is one after all.

The story of Zor holds a key to forgetfulness and also to remembering. It holds the power of light and darkness of self. A powerful and beautiful experience that holds the promise of uncovering to all who enter within it. Zor has often been used as a point of discovery for many initiates who are governed, not only by their own thought, but by the thought of others of what they would do if they were caught between the forces of light and the forces of darkness.

This story has assisted many in the Higher Worlds to understand the characters that they created, and in fact entered within, as they moved towards a greater uncovering of their real true heritage. Such is the story still to be told. The story of Zor that revealed to one initiate what in fact he still had to learn, and through his learning, so many others were able to grow.

Never look towards yourself as being only one. For you are indeed within the many experiencing what it would be like to be the one. Each one within each storyline allows for the entry and exit point to discover more and more about yourself, and in understanding what is and what is not, then you are ready to begin a new story and so on.

Zor was the beginning to some and the ending to others. It was and still is, regarded as one of the most beautiful "testing" places ever created by thought. To some, it has no ending, and nor do they want it to ever end. However, to others it has come and gone. It depends upon what thought you choose to have.

Chapter 5

The story continues ..

The City of Zor once existed. It was a place of beauty and peace. Its inhabitants welcomed travellers and initiates alike, who used Zor as their entry point into other realms of existence. It was the central city within an empire that had long held onto the ways of progression and open learning. Many initiates were introduced to long and arduous training sessions, so that they could ready themselves for what tests lay ahead, in places where they had never been before.

Zor was a place of reflection and, for some, a place whereby much could be learnt from many others who were in transit to other Worlds. It could be likened to a giant city, where buildings were composed of facets of light, rather than coarse materials that were often found in the Lower Worlds.

In human terms, it could be viewed as a central point within a giant grid. This grid was a network of channels that allowed movement through space via light stream travel. You cannot regard it as distance between one World and another, but rather through reflections of light, that permit entry into other Lands of varying frequency ranges.

The Empire of Zor was truly the paradise that many humans refer to as Utopia. It thrived on the progression and experiences of the travellers that came to these Lands, and held a beauty that no words would suffice to describe it. However, what can be said at this point, is that Zor was a place where you would not expect to find betrayal.

Opposites are a factor of life but not light. A journey through many Worlds offers up opportunities to gather experience and awareness of differing blueprints of life. Light is the main substance that one really is, and in saying that, then what happened in Zor is almost unbelievable .. but perhaps what is not expected, is the greatest test of all!

There was a central light that permeated the lands of Zor. It came from a central core. Within that central core lay the abundance of energy, being light and sound, that was required for Zor to exist in its present state of awareness. The central light was the benefactor of all movement to and from Zor via many channels through space that linked all Worlds together, to make Zor the place that it was.

The City of Zor was the central point within a cluster of Worlds that made up the Empire of Zor. Its custodian was a Higher Council of 12 that were delegates from 12 differing Worlds of life and light. It was the epitome of total respect, for much was gained through the input of each of the 12 Worlds to form a co-operative of existence.

All in all, it was the Utopian experience that formed a collective of 12 differing existences, all co-operating together, so that a greater awareness of light and life could be understood.

Some of these Worlds were of a denser nature, that allowed for their existence to formulate opportunities to exist within a life form that offered a more basic understanding of life, whilst others were in their transitional state of moving from the denseness of form into a higher range of light bodies. Each World was important to the next, for life was seen to be a precious gift, so as to establish a more direct link to the creative force that allowed for all life to flourish within many differing examples and opportunities.

The Council met regularly within the Central Chamber of Zor. This Chamber held the full regalia of light and sound of each of the 12 Worlds. It offered up to them an opportunity to hold their frequency of light and form intact, so that each member was able to be acknowledged by the others. It was within this setting, that the betrayal began.

When light and life join together, then darkness of thought enters in. For darkness is but a silent carrier of discontent, that waits in the shadows of one's intent.

Light and life have to come together to form a partnership of love, and through this love, comes the need to form a different partnership altogether. Life comes in many forms, centred mainly within two categories, the denseness of form and the body of light that revolves around a form that once was. This may be difficult to explain to one who is encased within a singularity body of matter. However, we shall attempt to do so..

Through the experience of existence, comes the relationship to a form, to take on the experience that is needed to be had. Form is relegated a number of coding sequences that allow for a structure of form to be designated, equal to the space/time experience required. Light is infused within a building block of life that is allocated a sequence of coding regulators, equal to its progression through evolution.

Within the Lower Worlds, the denseness of form is allocated, for the limited aspect of light allows this to be so. However, in the Higher Worlds form takes on a different example, with the lower aspect of itself falling away for the light to take on the fuller responses to the existence that it is within.

There are 3 levels of life within the storyline that we are sharing with you. The Lower Worlds, the Mid Worlds and the Higher Worlds. Each one bringing the necessary experiences to the Central World or what is called the Central Sun. Zor is an aspect of the Central Sun, taking on the main caretaker role of light and sound, so as to allocate to multiple Worlds of existence, the opportunity to relate together as "one", for the "one" is the prime source of light.

The formation of the Council allowed for each sector of space to be allocated an opportunity to invest in a collective experience with the many differing life forms that occupied each sector. This was done through an exchange system, whereby carefully selected representatives of each sector were sent to another sector, in exchange for their representatives, and so on.

This proved to be quite successful, as some of the differences within each of the 12 sectors were bridged, and a greater understanding of life within its different stages of evolvement was registered. Those who had journeyed to other Worlds returned home and shared their experiences and their stories with many others, who would never have had the opportunity otherwise. This practice was widespread throughout the Empire of Zor, and so much was gained. However, what is sometimes seen as a positive can sometimes become a negative, and it was through this arrangement that the betrayal was born.

In exploring Worlds beyond what one is used to and what has never been experienced before, an entry was born .. into a need, a desire to have the life that was not to be. Dissatisfaction grew from desire, from the need to find fulfilment beyond the life that had been given.

The stories and experiences from those who had travelled, who were ultimately called the "travellers", grew from what they had experienced to far beyond the truth of their journey. Stories are like that. Fashioned from fact, and then finding an element of non-truth, so as to create something equal to one's desire. And so, from the fundamental objective of sharing and learning from each other, discontent bred exaggeration and imagery, which ultimately led to the downfall of Zor.

Light was overtaken by darkness, and the City of Zor became the entry point for the revolution to begin. Where do we begin with a story such as this? How can we share with you what happened in Zor without leaving out a single fact. For to do so, would take away the impact of the devastation that totally destroyed what Zor stood for. It takes just one single action to open up the door to many actions, and that is what happened.

What was that action? It was within the need to have what one did not have. It was within the need to take what was not to be taken. It was within the need to create one unified World, and it was within the need to dictate the terms in order for it to happen.

The stages of existence are carefully impregnated through multiple cycles of experience. Thus Zor held many Worlds within its Empire. Each World held an evolutionary relationship to its environment and life experience. All was in balance with the Greater Plan, but that was not acceptable to those to whom believed that their Worlds should be different, and so the action of control over others was born.

The Higher Council met within a secret chamber. Four members were not present. The chamber shuddered under the weight of hostility towards they who had so much, from they who believed they did not. Resentment, envy and innuendo were the weapons upon that day. A plan was formed to create a united life form, drawing from the resources of those within the Worlds of light.

Evolution was discarded as dissent echoed its need for one master race of beings. The Central Chamber of Zor needed to be overtaken if the plan was to be successful.

That Central Chamber was within the City of Zor, and it held the full coding of all Worlds within it. A plan was formulated to invite all representatives of all 12 worlds to meet within the Central Chamber in the City of Zor. 144 in number.

With this plan in mind, then those from the 4 worlds who were not present at the secret meeting would be taken captive so that the overthrow of their Worlds could begin. The fabric of the plan was such that it would defeat even the most insightful and aware members of the Council. A plan of deceit that would draw to a close the current hierarchy of the Council.

And so, 8 members of the Council met in secret, whereby a plan was drawn up. Each sector would be offered the opportunity to extend their knowledge and resources into one commemorative expression of unity within the Central City of Zor. This would be a plan that would convince the 4 members that were excluded from the meeting to view this opportunity as a gesture of goodwill and progression for the future of the Empire.

You need to be reminded at this point within the story that the City of Zor was the central point that connected each of the 12 worlds together. Permission had to be gained to enter this City, for it was seen as a place that offered the necessary training and opportunity to initiates and travellers to progress within their understanding of the differing blueprints of life and light that existed within each World.

There was a very stringent rule that was observed, whereby each World was to be kept separate in order that their evolutionary progress be maintained. No-one was given permission to stay within a World that was not of their origin. Only trained travellers were able to enter into the various Worlds for a short time only.

The City of Zor, therefore, became the place that needed to be overtaken, so that this rule could be broken. It could be likened to the "hub" of the Empire. Many teachers and higher initiates lived within this City, and to overthrow Zor meant that both teachers and higher initiates alike had to be taken captive and disposed of.

The plan had to be executed swiftly if it was to be successful. Members of the 8 worlds met secretly four times over before the plan was acceptable to all. For the members of the Worlds of light would be hard to convince that the ceremony did in fact offer unity and not division, if any sign of deceit was displayed.

Thought is a powerful tool of diversity when confronting opposition, and through the power of thought of the many upon the Council, then the few stayed unaware of the Plan that had been put in place. All was ready to proceed, and nothing would ever be the same again.

The City of Zor opened up its gateway to every sector within the Empire for the unified gathering of all Worlds. Restrictions into Zor were lessened, so that many who had not entered into the City before could gain access for such an event. Representatives of all 12 Worlds gathered together for the first time to share aspects of their Worlds in comradeship and hope for future growth and progression.

Representatives from all Worlds entered into the City via a "transit regulator". A transit regulator allows for travel via light streams equal to the frequency range of that particular representative. It could be likened to a frequency dial that alters the ratio of energy equal to what it is carrying. Entry into Zor is through the correct entry point via "a hole in space".

Once the entry point is ascertained and accessed, then those who have entered are then taken to the Central Chamber, so as to take on a sheath of light equal to all others within the City of Zor. This sheath allows for the power ratio to be equalled, so that communication between all representatives from all Worlds is possible. The Central Chamber holds 124 access points of light. Therefore, allowing for the equivalent number of representatives at one time. Three times over, the Central Chamber was full.

It would be idyllic to present this story to you through the eyes of one who was there, and in fact, this is definitely the case. For I was there .. and I witnessed the birth and death of a revolution within Zor. A revolution that began with the need to possess what belonged to another, and ended with the destruction of Zor itself.

The primary facts are paramount to this story, and in saying this we need to remind you that the potency of the facts will never be experienced through the unravelling of the story, but in the very demonstration that these facts have resonated consequence after consequence in so many Worlds, including Planet Earth. These consequences do not contain the by-product of this revolution, but instead hold the very key to existence itself, as you know it to be. For "you" are the result of this revolution, and when you acknowledge this to be a fact, then this story will be your key to unlock the "real" you.

What happened in Zor is still resonating within your life. It is in the promise of tomorrow without remembering the yesterday. It is living within the moment instead of living within every moment that you have ever experienced. It is in the search for the ending without ever remembering the beginning.

It is the creator of your life, whilst not allowing you to remember your light. The simplistic response to such a profound explanation would be to remind oneself of their own reality, that does not align with a story such as this. However, within this simplistic approach, your life will continue on with the sameness, and this story will be only a temporary measure of interest and perhaps amusement. However, to all who are responding to these words, then listen carefully .. your lives are the result of the past, but have nothing to do with the future "you".

History has a way of repeating itself over and over again, and the cyclic aspect of this story is no different. For Zor was the product of change, not change for the better but to its very detriment. The idyllic lifestyle that was had by some and not by others, surely is the indictment of life as you would know it upon Planet Earth. It is the fundamental relationship of "what is" against "what is not". This very statement is the basis of truth within the rest of our story. Not the story of the lies and deceit that came from the overthrow of Zor, but in the restructuring of desire that came afterwards.

Zor was the Empire of many Worlds. It was fashioned upon the blueprint of evolution, from the denser life forms into the fabric of life that contained higher frequency life forms that were made of light. The evolutionary aspect of awareness allowed for each World to learn and integrate together in a unified and united relationship of awareness and acceptability of all variable experiences of existence.

When is the point when the desire for more than you have becomes an obsessive need to take rather than to receive? To cease to learn from another, but substitute it with the need to conquer and possess. There are no more questions to be asked but instead only a tyrannical expectancy for all to listen and to follow.

Singular life within the Lower Worlds is structured upon variation of thought and expression. It is the epitome for all to follow. Within singular life the need for evolution is necessary, for without evolution life cannot be maintained. It is as simple as that, and with that thought in mind, we can now return to the story of Zor and its subsequent downfall.

Chapter 6

The 8 members of the ruling Council met for the last time within the sanctity of the Central Chamber. Their presence was duly noted by those to whom stayed loyal to the plan that was now being put into action. This plan became the stalwart of the promise of what was to come, but they did not take into account that the future had already been run and their plan was doomed for failure. Let us take a moment to review what has been said.

The future has already been run, that is a fact. Within all life comes possibilities, and within each possibility it has an outcome. Each outcome is measured against what is required for the next anticipated outcome and so on. Eventually a pattern of mastery has taken place, and the beginning has led to an ending, without the beginning realising this fact.

What happened in Zor is happening within your lives. You are the reflection of what did indeed happen, and you are now viewing it from the vantage point of living it through one of the possibilities upon Planet Earth. That may seem difficult to understand, but in fact it is the very result of what did happen that did not work. Therefore, Zor can be viewed as an experience whereby so many wished to overthrow "what was" so that what "was not meant to be" could be the victor.

The point to all of this is that the future has already been determined, for if it was not so, then the Central Suns beyond Zor could not exist. They are the result of the perfect law of unified existence. There cannot be a beginning and an end, but instead there are multiple possibilities that can be moved through, so as to have the experience of imperfection.

So much for the need to find revenge within oneself towards what is deemed injustice. Instead it is in the experience of imperfection and one's response to it that determines the next possibility. All possibilities have reached their final conclusion, so that the next set of possibilities can occur.

As in the lesser, so it is in the greater. The Empire of Zor was imperfect, and in being so, was eliminated. Why was it eliminated? It was eliminated because the future had no need for it. It is as simple as that.

However, we cannot finish there, nor do we have a need to, but instead we wish to dedicate this story to "what was", and in doing so, allow you to view the reflection of what happened in Zor as being the very core of your own existence and your relationship to who you are.

You are indeed being shown the imperfection of existence within the singularity aspect of evolution. When you understand this, then the story of Zor will unfold your life as well as the purpose to it. The complexity will disappear as a more powerful vision of what lies beyond the "you" is shown. You will become a traveller through a possibility, rather than a victim or victor of it.

There are no victims or victors within life. There are only experiences to be had within the network of variables. That may seem somewhat devoid of sensitivity, but facts do not hold sensitivity, but instead are aspects of what is "real". To believe in who "you" are is to find solace within your belief of what you have created. Zor was like that. A place of splendour and wonder for some, and devoid of opportunity to another. It depends upon what one wants to see, rather than what is there to see.

We have not deviated from our story at all, but rather we are weaving the reason for it to be told. You may choose another method of enquiry through other stories that have been told, but we are bringing to you the opportunity to view yourself within the story, and why the story had to be told at all. Truth can no longer be given its entitlement as being the provider of inspiration without first being tested.

The question is .. how does one test truth?

For whoever is asking and whoever is answering, is the source for truth to be tested. In knowing this, then the story of Zor is an expose of your life and not the life of others, if you care to find the truth. However, if you read it as a story that belongs to another, then you will never find the truth at all.

Zor was a place of beauty and splendour to me. It held the resonance of light and sound that created images of what was possible. Within the centre of the City was a monument to all Worlds that made up the Empire of Zor. This monument could be likened to a fountain. It held 12 resonating frequencies which were seen as energy light streams that constantly flowed from this "fountain". All who saw it were drawn to its powerful resonance of love and unity.

Many within your World have spoken of "the fountain of youth" where the essence of everlasting life can be found. It is within this reflection, it is within this remembering, that this fable has been formed. However, this monument did not stand for the cessation of ageing, but instead it stood for the recognition that all belongs to the "one". The "one" essence where all life comes from and all life returns to.

It may be difficult to understand that the experience of life is to be infused with many tests of endurance. It would be so easy and simple to live a Utopian existence whereby all live in harmony and love. However, harmony and love is the fallacy of progression and evolvement. For what is harmony and love to one is not to another, and that is what our story is based upon.

There will come a time when the desire to go beyond what you believe in will occur, and when this happens, there will be a requirement to move towards a completely different experience altogether. How you approach this opportunity will show whether the cycle of experience within that possibility has been completed or not.

The intent behind the need is the entry into the next opportunity to move beyond where you have been or whether you stay within the same experience, rotating the sameness over and over again. The mask of illusion slips occasionally within a few, just long enough for them to view the "real" within themselves. If this is an ongoing proposition with the intent to reveal a greater prospect of remembering, then what is deemed the "future" becomes their now.

The records show that creation came and went. All was accounted for. However, within this very aspect of memory, came something that allowed for creation to be told for the second time. The formula for existence, as we have mentioned before, is the base of all life through the building blocks that are formulated via a Greater Plan. When life has been given the formula to exist, it also has within it a formula for non-existence. This formula allows for life to have a full range of experience before it is reversed into completion.

Such was Planet Earth. It has come and it has gone. However, how can this be? You believe you are existing within this place and you believe you are very real. What you are seeing is a mirror image of what has been. A reflection of what did happen, but is not happening now. Your existence within it is through a program that has re- activated life as it was upon Planet Earth in its lesser example. When we speak of a lesser example, then we need to explain:

All life exists upon 7 levels of existence. This we have already explained to you. However, you are existing within a program of life that has been reconstructed for the sole purpose of experiencing life upon Planet Earth within the aspect of what it was not. Hence, what did not work in the original creation. For life within creation held a formula to allow what did not work to be held within an 8th chamber/level.

This level allows for many to come and experience the opposite to what creation was really like. This comment is, of course, controversial to say the least, but yet accurate, and we wish to prove it to you.

Creation allows for growth. All life has a value system of survival that operates an internal monitor that allows for division to compensate for destruction. Not only through life threatening viruses and diseases, but also through the fragmentation of thought, so that what is created can be maintained.

When creation first came into being, it was given an external monitor system as well as an internal one. Thus life could be maintained, but yet held options open for advancement. What was created was given three operatives to follow. These three operatives were in line with each other and maintained the power ratio required to permit creation to follow a format of opportunity.

Hence creation became its own creator, establishing an open policy of following three variable operatives, so that it could follow a beginning and an end. A beginning and an end are only viable when there is a recognition that what was begun could never be held in stasis, but instead held the necessary advancement protocol to find an ending. Simply speaking, creation had a journey to follow. It was endowed with a requirement to always move towards evolution, ever changing and yet always surviving beyond where it had been.

However, if you look objectively and with no bias or fear, the 8th chamber holds very little opportunity for advancement. You will no doubt find a very powerful argument at this point and state quite emphatically that great progress has been made within the medical, scientific and technological fields, and in fact that is true.

What you do not know is that these qualities have been taken from the original creation and have not been created in the 8th chamber at all. They were re-located at various time intervals in order for the program to relay an account of what was invented and discovered.

The piece de resistance to all of this is to state the following fact: "Nothing new has been created in the 8th chamber". The original creation was open to all thought, so that the beginning and ending could eventually meet. However, anything that has come into the 8th chamber from beyond it, is met with intense scepticism and resistance .. for change is a powerful enemy and thus must be met with great opposition.

We have made a powerful statement when we spoke of the reality of your life being only a programmed image of what did not work within the original creation. Reality is one's measurement of dependability and security, and to even speculate that your reality is but an illusion, would no doubt create a rather powerful response. Before anger or even dismissal of this fact sets in, perhaps you would allow yourself to keep reading ..

Ask yourself the question: "What do I want from reality?" If your answer is "dependence upon what I have been taught to believe in", then the rest of this story is already lost to you. If, however, you have answered "to take me on an open ended exploration of possibilities and probabilities", then you will find that the rest of this story is for you.

To all who have stayed, we will continue .. The secret to all existence everywhere can be found within yourself.

You are the microcosm of a macrocosm. You are the lesser of the greater, and yet even within the lesser lies all that the greater is endowed with. You are the traveller or initiate that is viewing the journey through life via an internal register, rather than an outward reflection of what was. When you know this fact and believe it, then you have opened up the greatest story of all. It is the story of "you". You being the operative word to describe the real you. Your life is a chronicle of the past. It is a journey through the past that will offer to you many challenges, but will also provide you with opportunities to advance your awareness of both yourself and the life that you find yourself within.

You are living within an echo of what was, and when you become more and more open to your own real self, then the real sound of who you really are will enter.

You have entered into the 8th chamber for a reason. Surely, it is time to find what that means. Within the element of light there is always the experience of life. What is life, but a fabric of awareness that is fashioned according to the paradox inverted into it. Life and light are but the same, except through the awareness that they are not, which simply relates to the story at hand and the relationship of one's real self to the illusionary value of separation from it.

The 8th chamber is the quandary that you are currently within. Your exact response to your life will determine how you view the paradox of your journey through life. If you offer to your life an unlimited opportunity to discover what the 8th chamber is, then you will go beyond the boundary of illusion and enter into a reality that will open up a spectrum of new experiences.

You have entered into your World with all of the residue of what has been, so as to reconstruct the past through the advantage of knowing the future. The real you exists within the future, not within time as such, but within the future beyond where time once was. Why do you need to reconstruct the past, and what does it have to do with the story at hand? The answer to these questions are within the story of Zor, and the 8th chamber is the opportunity to view the real story, rather than the cover version through a fragmented program.

All initiates are expected to enter into the illusion of separation from their real selves, so as to find order within disorder, peace within chaos and awareness within deceit. Therefore, the story of Zor is the mainframe of opportunity through the program within the 8th chamber. It opens up the memory of Zor through the reflective images that have created the program of creation.

When the story of Zor is opened up through the program for each initiate's response, then the test has begun. How one views that test will determine the result. Let us now return to the very beginning of our story, whereby many initiates have not returned home. They are deemed to be "lost" to the program of life, through their very need to embrace the past as if it was their home. Their reluctance to remember the journey at hand has brought to them only a need to belong to the image of the past, thus establishing a desire to belong to the memory of Zor, as if it was real.

Let us establish a fact. Zor did exist, as the story dictates. However, it no longer exists, but the memory of it does. That memory is the training ground for many initiates, so as to determine their suitability for future opportunities.

When an initiate does not return home, then others are sent to find out why. Hence, the Dream Chamber allows for many to enter into the past in order to relocate initiates and assist them to come home.

The difficulty lies within the resistance of initiates to implement new opportunities to leave behind their need to belong to a program of the past. They have not only embedded themselves within the program, but have responded to the memory of Zor by implementing the negative value of this memory into their programmed lives. This has a compounded effect, not only through the activation of the memory of Zor into the program, but utilising Zor to empower their human memory shells.

The effect is catastrophic. There is an immediate activation of energy from the memory of Zor, giving forth energy imprints of characters that rely heavily on recognition of their reality through the program shells.

This may sound a little complex, but it is not. Indeed, it is simply the memory of the past program becoming its own reality, and activating the memory of Zor into a reality state also. Two memories coming together to empower each other. The initiate is totally lost at this stage.

The two power points magnetise each other, so as to protect the past. Anything new is completely rejected, so as to maintain the status quo.

There is a junction whereby light and life exist together. This junction is the main theme of the next segment within our storyline. It is the epitome of the Central Chamber, and indeed features strongly both within our explanation and the story still to be told. The exact location of Zor can be found within the nexus of oneself, insomuch as recognising that "you" are the entry point beyond the program of life. There are multiple examples to back-up this statement, and indeed we wish to use some of them in order to demonstrate this fact.

"You" are the result of the past. The past has come and gone, but "you" are still current. Why is that? What is it that makes up "you"? Are you the memory to which has been the mainstay of so many? Indeed, you are not. But who are you? What is the component that makes you the point of reference in measuring the past? All of these questions are highlighted in the story of Zor and the overthrow of all that Zor represented.

The answers, however, exist within your now. For "you" are the result of Zor. "You" are what happened, but "you" are not the reason for it to be so. Let us explain: Zor was a place that bears no reference to your life, or so you believe. It was a World far removed from the World of your reality, or so you believe.

You awake to a new day that offers up untold opportunities to discover more about the World in which you live, or so you believe. But what you do not believe .. is that your reality is "make-believe", and does not actually exist. If you can touch it, then it is real, if you can see it, then your vision describes the detailed evaluation of what is your reality, and so on.

However, with that in mind, you need to remind yourself that reality is one's own measurement of the past, and we have just spoken about the past as being the result, rather than the actuality of events. The source of all life is through the obsolete value of memory. Memory being the opposite of the real. What "has been" versus what "is". Your question is valid if you are asking "but how can memory be viewed if we are to understand what is real, and what is real contains no memory at all?"

Memory is the classic version of the past, being the gateway for what is to come. But what if all has come and gone, and all that is left is what is real? By the very nature of the past, all is seen to have come and gone, but in its true essence, the very point of observation of what "is", shall uncover the journey of "all that was not".

You are what has been. You are what is not. What is real is all that is left when the past is removed. That is simple in itself. But what is not simple to perceive is that "you" are the result of the past, but are not the past at all. The past being the observation point of what is not. What is not being all that is away from what "is".

The real is the essence of one's origin. What "is not" is the journey away from one's origin. That journey is the exploration that is called life. Life being the sum total of the "you". Your life is the result of what is not, of what has come and gone, and "you" are having the experience of when it occurred. It is that simple!

Now we need to address the most important fact of all. This journey is not your journey, but is a journey that someone else had. You are here to explore what did happen, but has never happened to you. For you are within a program that is linked to an "old" journey that was sent out from the essence of a Central Sun, completed itself, and the Central Sun has moved on to a greater aspect of itself, within another Central Sun.

All you are doing is viewing when the journey did occur, as a matter of discovery beyond where you have ever been before. Hence, the testing ground for the initiate, who has never journeyed here before, but has entered into someone who has.

There is a composite value in all of this. A human being, indoctrinated with the memory of life, and the initiate who has entered into this memory. However, the question remains "what does Zor have to do with this fact"? And the answer is simple – Zor is the result of whether the initiate was successful or not in integrating life and light together.

For Zor is the ultimate test to determine the power of the individual over and above the memory of what one truly is, and throughout this test the forgetfulness often belies selfishness and resentment towards all encounters with the memory of such a test. How best can one view the result of a journey thus far, unless an opportunity to foresee what has or has not been learnt is upon the initiate. For surely there can be no further movement within a journey if there is no effective measurement. But what is a measurement but a point of reference that can be utilised as a tool of opportunity, rather than a fear-based life of resentment and unsureness.

You are upon a Planet that is a representative of the past: we have established that fact. But what has not been established is the reference point of your "now" within the entirety of the Zor memory. Your question would be "but what does Zor have to do with Planet Earth?" And this question understandably would qualify an answer that will ensure that our story from this point on, will be totally understood through your "now" and not within a paradox of inequity. For Zor exists within the space of occupancy that you exist within. You could liken it as being within the timeless, whilst you exist within time. It is accessed through time, but is not of time. Therefore, it is only for those to whom have the ability to enter the timeless who qualify for the test.

All others are simply the simulated memory shells of the past, or are those whom no longer wish to take the test. The point where we are at within the story will now hasten your enquiry into the "you", or simply your enquiry will vanish. It is all a matter of viewpoint. It is all a matter of being within the point of discovery or the point of denial. For, from this point onwards, the story takes on a rather formidable turn.

The first and the last is the measurement of the beginning and the end. However, within this fallacy, comes the very entry into the rest of the story. How the beginning began and the ending came to be is the story that can never be told. But what can be told is how it all works, and how the beginnings and the endings within the journey of existence come and go at periodic intervals, so as to provide the movement through the spiral of existence towards the final ending.

The story of Zor shall now be implemented, so that time as you see it to be is only a reflection of the story that will now be told in its entirety. All references to paradoxes will now cease, as the only reality shall be within one's memory of Zor. It shall be told through the memory of myself, not Diane. I feature upon the first page of the story, and I shall feature upon the last. Others will take up throughout the story, to allow different vantage points to be registered, but all in all, it shall be shared through the memory that I have of the time I spent in Zor.

It will also be narrated through a current interface with the memory, as if I was living it within the now. This will be so because of the need to bring the power range of the memory into a more vibrant and emotive narrative for the reader to experience, and especially for those to whom have the memory of Zor just beneath their current human consciousness.

The story of Zor now begins. Wherever you are reading this story, sit back and remember ..

We were seated in a semi-circle to commence our first lesson of the day. There were 12 of us that had gathered together to enter the first initiation, and so upon that day it all began.

Questions rose up within me of what could be expected, but of course, my inquisitiveness was only a need to be ready to meet any challenge that would come my way. This need to anticipate any given opportunity or requirement of myself and others, was, even upon this day, one of my weakest flaws. In light of this, I readied myself to begin the first of many initiations that would determine my acceptance or non-acceptance into the greater test of entering into the Lower Worlds, and with that thought in mind, my teacher entered the room.

A manifestation of light through a sound wave that is commonly used by the higher teachers was sent into the room. My senses quickly picked it up as being a multi-layered sound that came from an obsolete galaxy that existed millions of years ago. That sound was re-created to assist in the exploration of existence of long, long ago.

By the standards set before us, we were required to enter into the sound and relate examples of life forms and evolutionary patterns within a time and non-time variance. Whilst this sounds quite difficult, to the initiate that wishes to enter into a distant, obsolete and untried realm, it is imperative to recognise and display an understanding of such a place. Distance is an illusionary aspect of relativity between one place and another. Thought is the transport, and the traveller relies upon the thought to get them there.

The key to thought is the desire to have it. If there is no desire, then there is no thought, and there is no movement at all. The intent is the fabric of destiny after all, and through the intent all is possible.

Time is the delay mechanism of thought, for through time, thought has to have a multi-purpose to exist. For example, to exist within time is to know that time exists. In recognising that time does exist, then there has to be a memory to which one relies upon to demonstrate the passageway of time.

Throughout the Worlds in which time is the requirement for existence to begin and finish, then time itself has to provide evidence that it exists. This is done by demonstrating itself through multi-layers of possibilities and probabilities that orchestrate opportunities to exist within differing examples. If these examples only occur once, then time cannot be recognised.

However, when they occur over and over again through a rotation of cycles, then time becomes the paramount observation point to each opportunity that exists. Time being the main provider of reference, rather than each thought being totally new. For what is new can never reach its potential through time if it does not become old first. This is called the evolutionary code of existence. It does not occur through many realms, but is usually activated within the lower, denser worlds for matter to exist within.

Such is the mission of opportunity that now faces me, for I along with others have been offered an experience within a Lower World that once existed several billion years ago.

It's imprint variance has established a link-up with other cycles of life within the same galaxy, and these cycles of life have now completed their need for existence. By being shown the imprint of life within the Lower Worlds, then I would be able to establish the formula that is far from being completed, that offers new life to other levels of space upon a different dimension.

Dimensional space being recognised as "many within one", with each dimension not relaying the content within itself to other dimensional levels.

This establishes a singularity code of existence upon each dimension, which allows for creation to maintain the singularity version of itself. New creative modules are then implemented once a cycle of life has been extinguished upon a dimensional level, and so on. Therefore space as such is an ever-present moving experience that offers endless opportunities for existence to come and go, according to the ratio of sound within that particular sector of space.

The difficulty lies within an imprint of life that is deemed obsolete, being brought back to life within its imprint value and utilised as a training ground for initiates. Whilst the memory value of it is imperative to the success or non- success of the test, the creative module being utilised upon other dimensional levels that is still active, can at times interface with activated imprints of life. When this occurs, a junction of "what has been" and "what is" creates an entry and exit point within space. A difficult and dangerous situation can occur, but this is also part of the testing process of the initiate. Can they withstand any other dimensional activity encroaching upon their designated sector of space?

Many overlays of memory are always valid within an imprint of the past. These overlays allow for each initiate to incorporate a different task within a variable number of possibilities in order to find one reference point in which to move forward from. The complexity of sound within a time variable imprint of the past is one of the most difficult tests of an initiate before taking on a pure light form. It is to validate whether an initiate is ready to move beyond form by becoming immersed in one of the densest levels of form that can be encountered.

It would be too easy to re-visit a place where one has been a long time before, and so a totally different place is chosen where none have ventured before.

And so, this may explain to you the purpose of the test of light through a sound wave that was just given to us. It was to question our knowledge and understanding of sound waves of light within a long since departed galaxy, and as I have just explained, the need to understand the intent and purpose of such a place is a necessary requirement to being accepted into the final test of form and sound.

I have elaborated my position within the selection process, but what I have not done as yet is to introduce myself to you. My name matters not, but my presence of light does. I represent a collective that is based upon three structures of sound. Each sound is relative to the next, and so a three tiered energy structure is available to me.

My form is a base of light, but with a singular consciousness that is connected to a mainstream collective consciousness. In other words, I am able to express through a singular example, but I exist within a collective network of light that determines my next opportunity.

You could liken it to a large stadium filled with people all listening to the same sound. When the sound changes, then it is apparent that one of the collective is now undergoing a different experience. This is not accurate in actuality, but can be viewed this way in the symbolic sense, for I believe that it shares the common denominator that is applicable.

A collective sends out one part of itself to have a singular experience for the good of the collective. When the experience is completed, then the collective adjusts to all experience that has been experienced by one aspect of itself.

You could parallel this experience to your mode of reference via an organization, religion, country or family unit. What happens to the lesser affects the greater. What happens to the greater, affects the lesser. It is no different. Nothing can be experienced without an effect taking place.

I have been chosen, along with 11 others, to represent the collective to which we belong. If we are successful then we shall enter into the Lower Worlds through a main viaduct that links up with the Main Chamber, where the garment of light is discarded so as to take on a matter body.

The solidarity of sound is implemented through 3 viaducts within this chamber. Each sound allows for a reversal of frequency to be instilled so that forgetfulness can be maintained, in line with the nature of the test. This in turn relegates the next entry into the timeline that the test aligns to. It is imperative to note at this point that the entry and exit points within the timeline that incorporate what is termed the timeless, is the main point to what we are now referring.

Can the influence of time that has once been, but is no longer, re-arrange the value status of an initiate? What the initiate has to remember is simply to exist within the total structure of sound that implements many and variable opportunities that incorporate the mainstream aspect of life but not light.

Can the wheel of opportunity turn and turn again in the initiate's favour, or will it relegate the sameness of each program that has no ending, but always reverts back to the beginning? That question orchestrates our next point for you to ponder upon.

Courageous but impetuous and obstinate are the tools of a fool. Each of these responses reflect a movement towards failure. Courage brings about boldness. To be impetuous is to take a step into the unknown without the wisdom of knowing why. When one is obstinate, then they never question their motives, but instead resist all assistance to enter into any state of being. When this occurs, then one is totally without credence, and the old programs become the master of self, without even a glance towards another pathway that is awaiting.

The openness of enquiry into what the Lower Worlds represent altered my entire awareness of how I would respond. It was too easy to relate to places where I had been. Memories of powerful energy alignments within so many Worlds in which time was non existent. And yet, what was being instilled within each one of us opened up an entry into a totally different range of responses that were so different and so powerfully divisible, compared to where we had been before.

One would expect to enter into a lower frequency ratio through the journey beyond one's mind, beyond one's concept, before entering into a higher energy range of awareness. However, this is not so. In fact, the Lower Worlds with its denser frequency ratio are not entered into before the initiate has experienced the higher accord firstly. It is easier to "be" than to "not be". For what is true and real is the foundation of what one truly is. When entering into a denser illusionary energy state of awareness, then the test becomes extremely difficult. So much so, that many fail, over and over again.

The formula for existence and non-existence was to be our test. We were to become influenced by non-existence that once had been and now was no longer. That was the difficult part of the test, for the delay ratio within time would become our master. Time therefore dictating our next response, rather than our response dictating the event to come.

Time holds all memory of existence. To enter into time simply means that one has entered into non-existence. That seems to be quite contradictory in itself, but in truth, it is not. It is simply a paradox in action. I will explain ..

Whilst one exists within time, then they are within the image of existence, with memory dictating one's reality. However, whilst this is only an image, when one is immersed within time then they are unaware that this is so.

They are totally within its power of thought that it is still existing, and yet to one who knows the truth of its existence then time becomes only a paradox, rather than a reality. Time and timeless become one within a greater understanding of what the test holds, and the realisation that time is an illusion holds the key to understanding non-existence whilst occupying the image of existence.

To become ready to enter into the Lower Worlds is no easy task, as I found out. For to draw upon all that I had been through the collective of experience and through the sub levels of my own experiences, did not allow the true nature of the test to come, to be understood at all. I was shown that eagerness was impulsiveness. Confidence allowed for self-belief rather than the wisdom of non-belief. To remember and yet to forget became the fallacy of it all. How could I forget and yet remember? That was the difficult part, and I spent so long preparing myself in the art of forgetfulness, whilst maintaining the remembering, that I felt that I would never be given an opportunity to even begin.

My mind goes back to when the lesson was first presented to me of duality of awareness: that is what it was termed. To hold a dual frame of existence and non-existence. This was the stumbling block for many of us, and it took a long, long time before we even began to master such a feat. The lessons were long and arduous, with a dual thought always operating via a sound wave of interference, that simulated what would happen in the Lower Worlds.

If you could imagine a sound that was so sweet, so beautiful, suddenly being infiltrated with a different sound that distorted the original sound, then that is what happens. The original sound is forgotten under the weight of the current distorted sound. However, if you remember that the original sound still exists, but exists within a different frequency that as yet you are unable to connect to, then the distorted sound is accepted, for you know the truth that the original sound still exists.

The lesson continued ..

All is within one point. All is seen beyond that point as being the reality, when in fact it is not. Within reality there are divisions of thought. Thought that offers a variation of realities, with each one being an observation point of awareness, until one reaches the next and the next, and so on. Whilst the need exists to view beyond one point, then reality shifts through the observation that it is so. All is within reach when one point is seen to be the entirety of all that "is" rather than reality being relegated to the awareness stream of multiple thoughts.

A rather complex lesson, and yet one that needed to be totally entered into, rather than to be understood. When you entered into it you were aware that it was all that existed, but whilst you believed you understood it, then you needed to experience multiple shifts of awareness in order to validate your understanding.

One point of existence was all "that was" and "is". That lesson became the cornerstone to all that I learnt from that moment on. Whilst I believed in myself, then I believed in the observation of who I believed I was, rather than the real truth of existence of what I really was.

A journey is the illusionary movement of awareness that takes us all from one illusion to another, and what is the point of the journey? Why it is to gather back the real truth from the illusionary image of movement away from the point of existence. To detach from one's own identity, whether it be within a collective identity or within a singular one, is the most important aspect to completing the journey.

Within that detachment therein lies a discovery that the journey itself is only a thought that offers an opportunity to disclose what it would have been like if that one point was able to become aware of itself. For within awareness, therein lies separation.

To know that the journey has never taken place, nor ever will, except by the thought that it did, challenged me totally. For within my thought of my own existence and the struggle to obtain a greater commendation through awareness, I became somewhat resentful that I could not ever obtain recognition for what I had achieved, and wondered what the point to all of this was.

The lesson became intensified with my struggle to let go of my identity. My identity was immersed with memory of all that I had done and all those to whom had become near and dear to me. My teacher persisted, patiently, ever so patiently. I was told to view the moment of now, the past and the future without viewing it through myself. To let go of my need to belong to it. To know that the past, the now and the future existed without me. Only the one point existed. All else was the illusion of believing that I existed. The "I" was the component that did not allow the real truth to be seen.

A battle erupted within me. My need to believe in what I had achieved and what I had still to achieve offered great resistance to the lesson at hand. I felt a strength within me that offered no respite, but instead added to the weight of resistance to letting go of "me".

My teacher waited for my battle to end, and when there was no sign of it abating, only then was I taken into the point of the "one". How can I describe to you the point of knowing that all is "one"? I cannot. However, within this lesson lies the story of Zor, that takes you to the point of understanding that what is away from the "one", also belongs to it. All is within the opposites. If there were no opposites to observe, then you would not be able to know "what" they were at all.

My return to illusion, with the knowing that it was, allowed me to enter the Lower Worlds with the most powerful understanding of all.

I understood nothing. Within nothing, all could be revealed. There was never a time when I was not, and yet within my understanding of the "one", then I awakened finally to the truth. All "is", and beyond this understanding lies what "is not". The two opposing ends of existence, and yet both needing each other to exist. This factual deity of expression gave to me a final resting place within my struggle to find the point to which all belongs.

Zor existed within my mind as being a place where existence followed different possibilities. A central city had been created as an observation point to observe aspects of itself. These aspects were in fact then patterned into a distinctive format that allowed for a story to unfold. The story of Zor.

Did Zor ever exist, or was it a place that lies within a storyline so that singularity can understand what "is" and what "is not"? Was the "one" created to allow for a central point of observation to bring what was "real" into view? Not as a negative or indeed a positive, but instead to bring it into one point. For within the opposites all can be seen.

This understanding brought to me great pain instead of relief, for in believing that I was indeed a central figure in righting what was wrong, allowed me to view myself as a positive fighting the negative. I could no longer hold onto my need to right the wrong, to rescue the imprisoned and to surge forward upon a journey that would offer me a place as a warrior of truth, opposing all that was wrong. I was in fact what "is not" believing that I belonged to what "is".

If there was only one point, then all else never existed. It only believed it did. The journey was the illusion, but it is within the illusion that the "one" can be finally known. It can recognise itself. Whilst it is beyond this recognition, then the journey will continue .. through you and through me. The story of Zor was created to bring all into one point, and within that one point, lay the next step to the next experience of what "is" and what "is not".

Zor was an entry point to a greater discovery. It allowed for opposites to meet each other so that the night and day could meet for a new dawn. Whilst night and day stayed apart, then the two opposing ends of awareness would prevent a closure to occur. There would never be a new dawn, and nothing new could occur. Therefore, the journey was created so that many stories would show the truth of the "one".

What did happen in Zor? It is time that the story was told, so that the new dawn can happen in me, and I hope it can happen in you ..

Chapter 7

The sound of melodic music was heard coming from inside the Great Hall. I paused to listen, and felt the beauty of the melody. It was one of my favourite sounds. I marvelled at the way sound was created here. Not through an instrument of matter, but through a thought that allowed for the sound to be manifested for all to hear.

This was the central City of Zor, and I had travelled from afar in order to experience its wonders and beauty. It epitomised the power of its twelve Worlds through the sanctioning by the Council to finally allow these Worlds to share their wisdom and knowledge through a central point. That central point was the City of Zor.

Since that decision, the doorway to the City heralded many opportunities for those such as myself to learn from the collective of all Worlds within the Realm of Zor. It was indeed a most beautiful place to be.

The nights were long, but the sounds of laughter and joy were constantly heard. It did not matter that the light within this place was short-lived, for the Central Sun was only present for a short time before the night descended again.

Where I had come from, the light was present for the majority of the time, and it took me a little while to adjust. However, there was so much to see and so much to learn from this place, that each moment was treasured within the light of discovery.

One's vision can become clouded when it is engrossed in discovery of what it believes it needs to see. It becomes negligent in its awareness, and its vision becomes the very cloak to prevent the truth of what is happening to be seen. For Zor held a beauty unsurpassed in many realms, and through the need to enter into its beauty and the need to not see what lay hidden, became its power point, as the mask of oppression lay silently in the shadows, waiting for the right time to strike.

Oblivious to this fact, I spent much of my time in the Halls of Learning, listening to many travellers who had come from these Worlds. Some were able to demonstrate their abilities to master thought and matter, whilst others spoke of the difficulties that their World endured. Each of the twelve Worlds were represented through their ambassadors or selected travellers who had experienced life there.

I was deeply engrossed in the need to understand the powerful differences between each of the Worlds and how they co-existed, despite their differences. I had never located such a variation before and was keen to learn all I could before I had to leave. It mystified me as to why so little had been shared between them before now. It was becoming more apparent however, that a collective was forming, with all Worlds finding a representation within a central point such as the City of Zor. A positive approach, or so I believed.

A collective works when all share unconditionally what they hold, so as to promote a central power point. It does not work when an aspect of a collective disengages and alters the constant, so as to take hold of the central power point. When this occurs, then all sink into a central matrix that is governed by the powerful agent of control that has over- ridden the purpose for the collective to exist.

There is a Higher Mind that exists that alters the evolutionary pattern of each World. Within this Higher Mind lies the governing power to promote a unity or division, according to the progress or lack of that is currently operable. It alters the causal flow of energy that permeates a World or Worlds so that the equilibrium is maintained, and the evolutionary status is preserved.

There are many names given to this Higher Mind, but whatever name it is given, its function is the same. Cultures and beliefs have been born from so many interpretations of what it is, but all in all its function is the same.

When this natural occurrence is left unimpeded, then the cycle of progression is upheld. However, when it is interfered with by those who wish to uphold their own version of evolvement through power over others, then chaos reigns. This is what happened in Zor.

I took my place in the Main Hall and waited for the speaker to arrive. I was extremely interested to hear this speaker. He had travelled extensively and had interacted with those who were able to enter into disembodied states, so as to enter the molecular world of matter.

I waited expectantly for him to arrive. However, my wait was in vain for he never arrived, nor was there a reason given for his absence. Instead a different speaker took the stand and spoke on the collective mind: an interesting account, but one I had heard many times. Disappointed, I left the Hall, and it was then that I felt that something was indeed very wrong.

I stopped momentarily to regain my composure. To reassess the position and to rely only on my inner vision and not my outer vision. It was just as well I did, for had I taken just one more step towards the exit, I would have entered into a position of great danger.

Members of a class 4 collective from a neighbouring World were being rounded up by operatives from the security force. Something was wrong! Something was terribly wrong! When I speak about a class 4 collective, I am simply referring to a group of scholars that had a class 4 clearance to study within the City of Zor. Their classification was within the teaching field and they would not normally be regarded as a threat to the security of Zor. Why they were being rounded up was a mystery to me, and my internal senses told me to stay hidden from view until I could ascertain what was indeed happening.

Sometimes inquisitive minds yield results, and this was no exception. Some time earlier I had been upon a tour of the facilities in which the Great Hall resided. A tour guide had offered information about the disused corridors that lay deep within the complex in case of invasion or threat from other realms. He told me they had never been used, for Zor was a peaceful colony and the original speculation of invasion had long been discounted.

My curious nature was stretched to the point whereby I implored him to show me these corridors, and we spent quite some time together studying the layout of where they were, and indeed where they led to. I was about to use that information to my advantage.

I made my way to the central walkway that led to the stairway that went down to the 2nd level. I then entered the corridor that led to the back of the complex. This region of the complex was mainly used for storage and there were multiple levels of storage cells/rooms that numbered in the thousands. It was here that I knew the entrance to the corridors could be found.

I remembered the tour guide speaking about a numbering system code that was in place to locate the entry points of the corridors. My memory scanned the relevant data that we had spoken of, and the answer came to me. There were three entry points to be found. One corridor led to the transit point to other Worlds, another corridor led to the outskirts of the City and the third corridor led to a chamber deep below the City. The point was, which corridor did I want to use? I quickly assessed the position. If there was a take-over of the City, then the transit exit to other Worlds would have been overtaken. I could hide deep below the City, and perhaps find others who had done the same, but I would not know what was happening. My final choice was that I could take the corridor to the outskirts of the City and take my chances there.

In deciding upon that choice, I made my way to the storage cell/room that would lead me to my destination. I had no time to lose, for in the distance I could hear shouting and screams. I needed to escape now!

The rooms were coded into three groups. Those numbered with a 0 at the end, the second group all were numbered with an even number at the end and the third were numbered with an odd number at the end. Within each of these coded doors was one room that held the entrance to the corridor. The room I was looking for was within the odd number grouping.

The code breaker for the room I needed added up to 13, started with a 0, held all even numbers and ended with the number 1. I located the room .. number 04621. I entered inside and found it to be empty. There was no sign of a doorway. I started to feel anxious. Where was it? Sounds below me of people running. Voices raised. I must find it quickly! Think!

Suddenly, I remembered .. he spoke of the entrance being denied to any who were unable to use the power of thought. It was designed to be available to the Custodians of Zor, who were able to use their thought to manifest and manipulate matter. My vast training had also given me this ability, and so I quietened down my mind and concentrated on the opening to my freedom. A few moments went by and then I heard a sound. I opened my eyes to see just before me in the darkness of the room, an opening in the wall, just big enough to fit through.

I quickly entered the small opening and closed it behind me. I was in darkness, but at least I felt safe. On my hands and knees I crawled downwards for what seemed forever. In the complete darkness I felt alone, but yet I knew that I had no other option. The memory of the map came back to me, and I drew upon this memory to know that a large room should be close by. I was not disappointed.

After what seemed forever, I saw a pinprick of light ahead of me and eventually I came out into a large room. Light came in from high above, and indentations had been carved into the rock wall that would allow me to climb up towards the light. It was easier than I first thought, and before long I had located a narrow opening high above the entrance to the room. There was barely enough room to crawl along it, but I slowly made my way towards an exit that came out in the hills surrounding the City. I was free. I was finally free, but what now? That was the question. What was happening in the City? I needed to know.

My sense of relief was soon extinguished when I realised that the skies above were filled with incoming craft that were targeting different sectors of the City. Many buildings had already been destroyed and many more were suffering the same fate. Places of great solace and beauty lay in ruins and I felt helpless and alone in that moment. Who would want to destroy such a place that was so well known for its Halls of learning and its many wonders that defined the 12 Worlds to which it belonged? It was a place of peace, and yet its fate was ultimately destruction.

From my hidden vantage point deep in the hills, I wondered about my own fate. My survival depended upon my ingenuity to formulate a plan that would allow me to leave as soon as possible. I needed to let someone know what was happening. But in that moment, I did not have a plan, nor did I have any knowledge about those responsible, and why they were doing this. All I could think of was that I had come to Zor to learn about the collective aspect of life via the central point which was the City of Zor. However, what I was viewing was the senseless destruction of what had long been regarded as the idyllic place to reside, with peace being the main factor of its existence.

I do not know how long I had remained hidden, but what I do know is that I was witnessing the ending of one of the most influential and progressive places I had ever experienced. Sadness and despair overtook my initial fear as the power of destruction that lay before me relentlessly continued. My refuge became my prison as more and more craft landed beyond the City's perimeter. I dare not move or else I would be found. What had begun as a journey of discovery quickly turned into an ordeal that threatened my very existence.

When one is confronted with a situation that provides limited opportunity to disassociate from a situation, then and only then does the truth of their character emerge through their response. That is what happened that day. From fear, emerged sadness and despair. Then fear visited once more: to finally move aside so that courage and determination could take over.

A need for an immediate action is always accountable via the result. If no action is taken because of indecision, then one awaits the action of circumstance, or of another, and so on, to determine the result. Therefore, my decision was to take action and to not hand over the power of action to another. Thereby, allowing me to have control over my own fate through my own responses. In knowing this, it gave to me great courage and determination to move on, to move forward towards not only finding a way out of this place, but to also make contact with any others who have also escaped and were in a similar position to myself. Thus taking back the power over my own fate.

It is an amazing fact how strength and resolve returns so quickly when one takes back the power and control over their own existence. There is a recognition that a powerful resonance of awareness exists within each one when faced with challenges that go beyond their familiar perimeter of experiences.

I drew upon everything that I had ever been shown, ever been taught, so that somehow I could make a difference. I moved quickly towards the outskirts of the City, down the narrow pathways that many had so often used to view the beauty of Zor from high up above the City. All around me seemed so surreal, so different now. I adjusted my gaze momentarily from the City towards the skies above. There were hundreds and hundreds of craft entering through the portal that I had been transported through only a short time ago, but yet seemed forever.

I watched them carefully, looking for some recognition of who they might be, but I could find none. Each one landed in formation. Their precision was quite extraordinary. They obviously had prior knowledge of the central district and the area in which they had landed, for whoever was behind this invasion knew the central City of Zor extremely well.

Here I was, all alone, within a place that was known to be a peaceful colony that offered to all a place of learning, beauty and the inter-mixing of differing evolutionary life forms. You could not just enter the City of Zor without being granted a permit, for this place was well sought after by many scholars and initiates from many Worlds. It was unbelievable. I had studied so hard to be offered an opportunity to come here, and now all I wanted to do was to leave, but how?

To transmit a message on my messenger coil would take the frequency through the main central system, and of course the system would have been manipulated by those invading the City. More than likely, even before the first ships arrived, by those from inside the City that were supporting the invasion.

It was obvious that the success or failure of this invasion relied upon keeping all suspicion away from what was happening. That being the case, then the Central Communications Command Station would be manned by those involved in the deception, who were receiving and relaying messages as if there was no trouble at all.

This was the time that the invaders were most vulnerable. If the authorities beyond Zor were alerted before they had established full control of the City, then there was a chance they would not succeed. However, it would be foolish if I was to try and enter the City, for I would be immediately questioned and detained. However, if I could find a way to transmit a message via another communications system, then it was possible that their plan would be foiled. The obvious question was "how"? I sat down and closed my eyes, deep in concentration...

A silence engulfed me. The struggle between my outer and inner self ceased. I became whole again. I felt the wind gently caress my face. I was transported into my own inner kingdom that I had denied for so long. It was within this place that I had once made a mistake, so long ago. A decision that cost many lives.

I had struggled with my inner senses for so long, and instead had relied upon my outer senses that taught me so much. However, an imbalance occurred. I had stopped trusting my inner self, and no matter how my teachers had tried to encourage me to make decisions from within, I was reluctant to do so. It seemed ironic that I was faced with a dilemma that my outer senses could not find an answer to, so I had to finally turn inward again and trust.

My mind went back to that fateful time when I had to make a decision that involved so many others. A decision that proved to be wrong, and if I could re-live that moment over again, it would be all so different. Regret is part of decision making, so they told me. In choosing an action, then you have to accept the consequence. Action and consequence are partners. They are aligned to each other in everything that we do. It is so easy when an action leads to a consequence that can be altered or changed, but when it involves a choice that leads to life or death, then the power of that action and subsequent result cannot be reversed.

From within my inner self, I allowed the memory to unravel again. I was a Commander of a space ship that was sent on a mission to resolve disputes upon colonies within the region of Altar that was deep within the Citron galaxy. We had just entered that sector of space when we came across an outpost that seemed deserted, but was supposed to be populated by more than 10,000 colonists. Many were research scientists who lived with their families and others within a small colony. They were studying the remains of an ancient civilization, long since departed.

After attempting to contact the colony, with no success, we landed in a desolate and deserted landing bay that was used by those visiting the colony. We searched for signs of life for many days, but found none. 10,000 colonists had disappeared! Something was very wrong! I was out of communication range to ask how to proceed. Therefore I took it upon myself to make a decision based upon an inner feeling rather than use the evidence and facts that lay all around me.

My decision was to leave a small group of my crew behind with orders to keep looking for clues as to what had happened, and I would return back to the main home base for further instructions.

20 people were left behind with enough supplies until my return or the return of others. They were left with strict instructions to continue searching for clues of what had happened. However, upon my return with three other ships, they had also gone missing.

The search for the crew and the colonists was one of the biggest searches that had ever been conducted, with the mystery finally being solved when it was discovered that renegade factions from an inter-dimensional realm had entered via an unstable wormhole in space. This wormhole only opened every 30 rotations of the Central Sun for a short period of time. The colonists and the crew were never seen again. I wished that I had made a different choice that day. I became mistrustful of my inner senses, and instead relied more and more upon my outer senses. It was such a long time ago, and yet I had not let my regret pass.

My visit to Zor was certainly not ordained by myself. In fact, I was here because I needed to re-acquaint myself with my inner vision. To remember the inner pathway to one's real self. The tranquil and peaceful environment allowed for an opening deep into the recesses of memory, whereby it was supposed to heal and soothe the pain that was attached to memory.

The situation that I found myself in was certainly far from soothing! In fact, it had drawn up the memory of my failure to which I had tried for so long to forget. In order to find strength and resolve, I needed to place the memory that I had carried for far too long aside and once again enter into the inner sanctuary of my being. I needed to trust myself again! If I was the only one who could help in some way, then I had to forget everything that had happened such a long time ago, and re-focus. I entered into a state of inner calm. All sound ceased. I had re-entered a place where trust was my only ally. I slowed my breathing down to a point whereby I started to move away from my conscious self. Shapes and images played games before me, then slowly they were replaced by a more definable clarity that resurrected my memory of several days before... A lecture on the sound and images of thought.

We were given a demonstration on how sound transmits light waves and how thought is the carrier of that sound. Two highly developed initiates were brought in to show how thought transmitted sound through the re-adjustment of a mind ready to receive. It went beyond telepathy whereby one receives a thought that another sends, but is often limited by the distance involved. Instead this involved a highly concentrated sound wave that could travel immense distances. The power of the mind can manoeuvre sound. I had also learnt this a long, long time ago.

The positive attributes of relaying sound meant that acquired information did not need an artificial means of transportation. Many places that I had visited did in fact use this method, but I had never had a need to do so until now.

The irony of the situation became almost too much to bear. All around me was chaos: that was a fact. I was involved in an invasion of the most insidious and unsolicited kind against a City of great knowledge and great beauty. The sound of battle echoed throughout the Land, and I knew that I had only little time left to do something. That something meant that I had to disarm my memories of long ago, and take heed of all that I had been taught, and once again trust totally in my inner self.

Taking a final look around me to clarify that I was indeed alone, I closed my eyes. I centred my inner being upon a point of light. That light was to be my carrier wave to those whom I regarded as my mentors and teachers within the place that I called home. I drew upon the memory of all that I had learnt, of all that I believed in. The point of light became a vital factor within my communication. I drew upon the essence of my very being, which held my signature of sound.

The light started to vibrate. I held it steady and I sent a thought to enter into it. That thought held the images of what was happening in Zor. I empowered that thought over and over again until I was satisfied that the light was saturated with the message of attack against the City. I concentrated upon the light until it started to pulsate. The most difficult part was about to begin. I needed to accurately define the pathway that it was to travel, so as to reach those whom I needed to contact.

Slowly and carefully, I visualised my mentors and teachers. They who share a united collective mind, and who would hopefully be able to receive the message that I was sending.

Love was the most powerful frequency that would reach them, and so I thought of them with the memory of the love that I shared with them on so many occasions. I was ready to send. The light pulsated and started to rotate. I took a deep breath and then with all of my inner strength, I projected it outwards. It took only a moment, and then it was gone. I fell to the ground, exhausted. Emotion engulfed me. I shed emotion, not only for what lay all around me, but for all that I had denied for so long... the truth of the inner pathway.

I knew that I had succeeded in sending it, but whether the signal was strong enough to be received .. ? All I could do, was wait and see.

Anger, sorrow, joy and hope all became my companions. Each one told their story. Anger at the beauty that was senselessly being destroyed. Sorrow for the needless slaughter and suffering that so many were going through. Joy at finally being free of the heartache of memory, and hope that the tomorrows would show me a new way to be.

Selfless and selfish stood side by side. I cried for all existence everywhere, and I cried for myself.

I took stock of my situation. Whereas a short time before I was eager to be close to the City, I now knew that it was not safe to stay where I was. The City below me was in ruins. Hundreds and hundreds of ships had landed, and the skies had borne witness to the destruction that day. I set off to retrace my steps and head back to higher and safer ground to wait.

I cannot say that I was brave or indeed even clever at using an untried communication method, but I can say that in doing so I felt a sense of renewed empowerment over circumstances that I could not prevent from happening. That, in itself, was a feeling of accomplishment.

Amongst a collective mind there is a pattern that is created. It entitles each one to share and also receive. Each experience holds multiple choices of response. From the variation of responses within the collective, so much is gained and so much is learnt. All comes into one communal understanding.

However, when there is a need to divide the collective into singular aspects in order to re-evaluate the singular mode of response within it, then the journey of the essence takes on a different role altogether. Many lessons are learnt through both failure and success. How one responds to failure and success determines the next stage of the journey.

I have struggled for a long time within a singular experience with the need to hold onto failure. The accountability factor that designs what is still to be from where one has been.

The root cause of all response is from the central point of one's observation, according to the memory they wish to utilise upon the next step of their journey. Why tread the same pathway that leads you to the same outcome? It is obvious that the answer to this question is to take another pathway altogether. However, in doing so, then nothing is confronted, for memory has a way of following you, no matter where you go.

I reflected on why I needed to come to Zor. I was chosen to come to the Lower Worlds to experience the power of singularity whilst observing its readiness or non-readiness to enter into a collective. They said it was to be an opportunity to experience the Lower Worlds and singularity within a tranquil and peaceful environment.

As I have spoken of before, Zor was a composite of 12 Worlds that were all within differing evolutionary states of awareness. By the lesser opening up to the greater, then the lesser could begin to blend itself into a collective and subsequent higher frequency.

The 12 could come into the one. Each of the 12 held a sound. Each sound resonated to the opportunity to link into the next, and so on. Finally, the 12 sounds or frequencies were to come into one sound. Zor had then completed what it had to do. The evolutionary experience had been completed, and the next step for the "one" was to join another "many", and so the process went on.

Therefore, Zor was the epitome of equality. It was an experiment of light. All in all, Zor was the paradise of the Lower Worlds. In fact, it was the epicentre of the Lower Worlds that would eventually evolve into the Mid Heavens.

I saw the immense power behind the Greater Plan. Time stood still. The past, the now and the future combined to illustrate that beyond our need to exist within the framework of acceptability, lay an immense power source that was the overseer of all existence everywhere. It did not judge, but instead it watched and waited for each one to follow the pathway of their choosing and experience the result of that choice.

The choice that I had made was to leave behind a number of my crew within an environment that was uncertain. Within that choice, I believed that the colonists missing had a better chance of being found.

So, within a choice comes other choices that lead to the eventual result. I have always regretted the choices that I made upon that day, and in choosing regret, it led to many other choices that led to more regret, and so on, and so on. It is amazing how cumulative one action can be.

I was starting to understand why I had come to Zor. In viewing the power of the "one", I was able to see that my feeling of inadequacy and incompleteness was the illusion that kept the "many" from becoming the "one". Zor reflected the need to become "one" and yet it was being prevented from being so by those who believed in staying incomplete and singular.

I was a reflection of Zor, whereby the "many" did not want the "one" to exist. The conflict that I had held onto for far too long did not allow me to be within the "one" of the real of what I am. Who I believed myself to be became the master of the illusion that I had chosen to live within.

Trials and tribulations are there to show whether there is a need to stay within the incompleteness of self, and the journey to the Lower Worlds helped me to reach inside myself through my singularity expression here, in order to define my readiness or lack of to go beyond where I had ever been before.

I had entered into a character via forgetfulness, in order to find a continuation of the same or to find an ending. Who I became in Zor is not who I really am. The careful blending of the real me into the character within a storyline allowed me to take on memories that were not mine at all. They were designed to integrate the imprint of memory of singularity into a testing procedure, to see if in fact I was ready to move on from the place that I called home.

There can be a profound effect when one is asked to leave a place that they call home. A place where they believe they need to stay .. forever! However, you cannot hold onto anything. The point of where one is has to be within the oneness of all. In knowing that, in understanding that, then the journey continues. The lesson has been learnt.

The battle in Zor was reflecting the battle within myself. I had held onto a need to always be right. To reach beyond what I believed was expected of me and what I expected of others. I needed to determine that there was no right and no wrong, but all was a semblance of differences that eventually led to the same outcome. That outcome was the point of understanding that all led back to the point of origin, which was the source of "all". How we got there was determined, not through the experiences that we chose, but how we responded and learnt from those experiences.

The character that I had entered enabled me to view memory within a frame of fear and shame. In holding onto memory was the greatest obstacle of all, which often led to a cyclic and non-progressive point upon our journey, returning over and over again to the sameness of thought and action. Going no-where, but back to where we started.

Within the integration of the character with my real self, I saw that for far too long I had harboured guilt and sadness, with my ego self at the forefront instead of the background of many choices that I had made. A need to be right often leads to what becomes wrong. It is not in an action that an answer comes, but it is in the knowing that each action leads to a greater awareness; that choice is the greatest gift of all. For this gift allows us to learn and grow.

The simplicity of all experience is to make a choice, create an action and accept the result. If you do not like the result, then change the choice, create a different action and await a new result. Surely, this is the movement upon the journey back to the source of "all". And so, alone, amid chaos, within a City under attack .. I became aware of the true nature of myself. I was no greater or lesser than those who were attacking the City. They had made a choice which will lead to a result. All who made that choice would have to meet the consequences of that choice. How they responded to the consequences, determined the next choice that they would make.

The victims of their choice would also have their own choice of response. Whether that be fear, anger, confusion or even acceptance. Whatever choice the so-called victor or victim made would outline their next experience to be had. To view life from the lesser ego self is to maintain the need for survival. However, when one views life as a journey that encompasses different forms of existence within ever- changing worlds of habitation and opportunity, then and only then will the greater aspect of oneself reign supreme. All else falls away.

For life is but a journey through endless stages of experiences that open up the very core of one's real self.

I felt different somehow. A freedom of belonging, not to self, but to the experience of the moment. I looked out across the City and I knew that I had been sent here to observe the downfall of Zor! It was within this very knowing that I heard a voice ..

"Come back to us Amoen, for it is all over". I opened my eyes to see the wisdom and light shine from my teacher's eyes. He smiled as he held my hand. "The tomorrows will be different because of this day" he said. "You have found the peace that was so missing within you. Come, come and join us. There are so many who are waiting to hear what you have experienced.

You agreed to enter into the Lower Worlds to a place called Zor. It was a memory of a place that existed a long, long time ago. It was regarded as the epitome of creation. Its 12 Worlds were ready to begin a transition into a higher phase of existence. It was to enter into the "one". Not the oneness of its own experiences, but of all experiences within the Lower Worlds.

It is an unfortunate fact that change is not always welcome. When one finds a paradise that gives to them everything that they ever wanted, then they guard their paradise against all who wish to take it away from them. They did not want Zor to leave the Lower Worlds.

However, upon the journey .. whether it be within singularity of collectiveness, within form or formless, nothing can ever stay the same. All is upon a progressive movement of experience. When the need to stay within one experience is greater than the need to learn from that experience, an empowerment occurs to increase the depth of dependency upon that experience, and the journey becomes forgotten.

However, there is a natural law that intervenes. The greater always absorbs the lesser. That is the way of all life. What has been, that no longer needs to be, is the lesser. What is still to find its full potential draws upon what has already reached that point. It is in the knowing that the end has arrived, that marks the prophet from the follower".

I was sent to the mystical Lands of Zor. A place that existed a long, long time ago. The place where one finds what they are looking for. It was an inner reflection of the mind of all who go there. Zor was the embellishment of what was and what was not. It was as simple as that. How one viewed themselves was how they viewed Zor. It was not a place, but in fact it was a state of being.

A collective of differences, a realisation that equality did not exist as such, but through accepting what was variable and indeed different, allowed for the understanding that all life everywhere radiates a sound.

Within that sound, there is a recognition that the journey back to what "is" has to have boundaries, has to have differences, so that all experiences can be registered.

Light and dark are the symbols of extreme differences, and yet they also represent a relationship to each other. Whilst the awareness of the journey versus the need to not have a journey lies in opposite ends of experience, it also allows one to view the other, so that they can both experience what is and what is not in unison.

From the powerful to the powerless. From the truth to the non-truth. From the sound to the no-sound. All is "one". How we view the differences, how we respond to those differences, determine the next experience that we need to have. There is no right and there is no wrong. There is only a journey of remembering. When you wake up and know that, as I did, then the dream is over. The next experience awaits.

Whilst I had returned from the Lower Worlds, many had not. They had become the Master and Slave to their own illusion.

To all who are viewing this story .. Wake up and remember! This is only illusion. Illusion cannot be maintained forever. It is time to wake up. For goodness sake .. wake up!

We have come to take you home. It is time.

THE END

I see the illusion that is all around me, but I cannot see where I entered and where I may leave.

It has been so long since the beginning ..

where is the end I wonder?

The dream seems so real ..

have I been within it so long?

Help me to find the ending ..

for it is there that I shall find the Inner Chamber where the Flame resides.

The doorway opens to the Inner Chamber and I step towards the Flame of Remembrance ...

I awaken to find Him looking down at me.

His words were gentle and soft ..

"Welcome Home, we have been waiting for you".

Available Reading:

**The Journey Home
with Elonias**
Diane Swaffield

The Greatest Story Never Told
Amoen, Diane Swaffield

The Temple of Remembrance
Diane Swaffield

Upon the Sands of Time
Diane Swaffield

Available Viewing:

'The Illusion of Reality' Documentary
Written, produced & Narrated by Jason Swaffield

Online Resources:

eloniasfoundation.com
thetimecentre.com

www.ingramcontent.com/pod-product-compliance
Lightning Source LLC
Chambersburg PA
CBHW051434290426
44109CB00016B/1551